4-6-96

To Pastor Stan Buck

My earnest prayer is that the Holy Spirit will lead you into the heart of the message in this book, and that you will emerge in the grandest of all causes for the American Christian,

The United States a Discipled nation in this generation,

Your brother in Christ

Jim Russell

Foreword by Cal Thomas

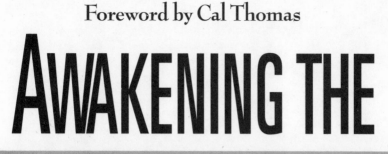

AWAKENING THE

Mobilizing and Equipping Christians
to Reclaim Our Nation in This Generation

GIANT

JIM RUSSELL

ZondervanPublishingHouse
Grand Rapids, Michigan

A Division of HarperCollinsPublishers

Awakening the Giant
Copyright © 1996 by Jim Russell

Requests for information should be addressed to:

📖 ZondervanPublishingHouse
Grand Rapids, Michigan 49530

Library of Congress Cataloging-in-Publication Data

Russell, Jim, 1925–
    Awakening the giant : mobilizing and equipping Christians to reclaim our
nation in this generation / Jim Russell.
      p.   cm.
    ISBN 0-310-20176-4
    1. Christianity—United States. 2. Christianity—Forecasting. 3. Mission
of the Church. 4. Church and the world. 5. United States—Church
history—20th century. 6. Church renewal. 7. n-us. I. Title.
BR526.R67   1996
277.3'0829—dc20
                                           96-6443
                                             CIP

This edition printed on acid-free paper and meets the American National
Standards Institute Z39.48 standard.

Interior design by Sherri L. Hoffman

Printed in the United States of America

---

96 97 98 99 00 01 02 /❖ DH/ 10 9 8 7 6 5 4 3 2 1

CONTENTS

FOREWORD

IN WHAT HAS come to be known as "The Great Commission," Jesus put discipleship at the head of a list of priorities to be practiced by those who would follow him. In our day, we have too often had other priorities. That is why the church of Jesus Christ lacks power, not political power, which is no power at all, but moral and spiritual power; the power to transform lives—our lives, and then other lives when they see ours have been transformed.

But we must start with ourselves before we can be of help to others.

One hears much these days about "apathetic" Christians and the need to be "more involved." Usually this is in the context of our national social and political ills. The question is not why more believers aren't involved in such things. The question is, why is there so much apathy? The answer is that there are too few disciples of Jesus Christ.

Consider those people and things that are important to you. Some people are addicted to ice cream or other seductions. There are some special friends with whom we like to spend time whenever we can. No one has to motivate an ice cream lover to go to the store and buy ice cream or to invite a special friend to dinner. Yet, we feel the need to be motivated when it comes to Jesus. Is it because we don't love Him as much as we do ice cream and our earthly friends? Do we find Him inconvenient? Would we prefer a "low-fat" Jesus who doesn't require us to be disciples?

The greatest authority on human relationships there ever was is Jesus Christ. Why won't we consult Him before we act? Why do we think that only big things and big names and big money are indications of the calling and blessing of God?

We begin with the big things when Jesus tells us to start small. If we are faithful in small things, He says, then He will give us charge over the bigger things. We prefer to start at the top and avoid the valley. So we seek to build big ministries. We concentrate on the presidency and ignore the city council. We get involved in campaigns to "reach the world for Christ" but have never met our neighbor. Jesus spoke about small things: mustard seeds, not oak trees; the last shall be first, not "We're number one," as the chant goes; the meek shall inherit the earth, not those with the best press agent; humility instead of pride.

Too often, we want to begin with transforming Washington, when we should begin by allowing ourselves to be transformed. Washington will be the last place, not the first, to experience the effects of such transformation.

One of the questions I'm asked the most is, "How did you get into so many newspapers, a national television show on a mainstream network (CNBC), and find a New York publisher for your latest book?" The answer is that I stopped cursing the darkness. I don't complain about "media bias." I do something to invade the territory and "occupy" it with the mind of Christ. People ask me that question because they think it is impossible to penetrate the "secular" media, thus fulfilling their own prophecy.

We have too narrow a view of the "mission field." We think it is a place that people go to, usually by plane and with a passport. In fact, if we belong to Christ, we are (or should be) missionaries, and our "field" is wherever God places us: in school, in the home, in our profession. "Go into all the world," said Jesus. That's not just the religious world, but *all* the world.

I have grown tired of believers who are always worried about the next "conspiracy" or decision by a government official they don't like. Don't they realize we are on the winning side? Why don't we start acting like it?

Satan's most effective tool is to get us to focus on what he is doing and not on what Jesus wants us to do. If he can direct all our energies toward putting out the social and moral brushfires he starts, he can make significant headway in the short run as he advances his agenda.

In *Awakening the Giant*, Jim Russell outlines how we became so impotent in the world and, more important, what we can do to turn ourselves around and face the Lord again. Jim is a man who literally puts his money where his mouth is. Rather than starting another "movement" or organization, he has focused on the small things and, as a result, the impact of his influence is growing.

First, in his family and business life, then through the Amy Writing Awards, which gives cash grants to writers who include biblical verses and wisdom in mainstream publications, and most recently in the revolutionary Church Writing Group Movement, Jim Russell has been a consistent and powerful tool who is being used by the Lord in the building of His kingdom.

Awakening the Giant is the blueprint for that work. Those who read it and heed its teachings can also be effective tools in the building of God's kingdom no matter how much "talent" they think they may or may not have, no matter the odds.

Jim Russell may not be on many people's "top ten" list of the most influential in building God's kingdom. That's okay. He's on God's list, and he's doing God's work. Read and absorb a book that is more than theory. It is ideas put into practice and finely honed into something that works.

Cal Thomas
Syndicated Columnist

ACKNOWLEDGMENTS

I WISH TO express my profound gratitude to the following people who opened the door of my mind to the idea that I could do a book and gently led me through the process.

Carl F. H. Henry, my cherished friend, who planted the seed several years ago with his astonishing statement, "You should write a book."

Terry Hart, prayer partner of the Amy Committee, who faithfully pressed for the book and supported it with his prayers.

Bob Briner, precious mentor, who was a catalyst in transforming the idea into the act of writing it and encouraged me through the entire process.

Lyn Cryderman, discerning coach, for his faith in initiating and sustaining the commitment by Zondervan Publishing House.

Phyllis, my loving wife, who listened supportively as I tested a thousand ideas against her wisdom.

Linda Blair, effective administrative assistant, who patiently taught me WordPerfect and suffered with me through the agony of lost copy.

Kathy, Vicki, Lori, Jimmy, and Amy—each of our children—for becoming what we hoped and prayed they would be.

PROLOGUE

IMAGINE THE YEAR 2025. You are in a state of unimaginable joy and anticipation. The news arrived by special courier just two days ago, and you have not yet fully accepted the reality of its truth. Its meaning was clear, the message brief. Beautifully hand-written in ink on the finest parchment, first the announcement, then the instructions.

"You have been selected to present to our heavenly Father the First Quarter Century Report of the spiritual condition of the body of Christ in America. On the first day of the coming new week you are instructed to remain at home. You will be spiritually transported to a heavenly kingdom. There you will be met by two angels of the Lord. They will usher you into the presence of the King of kings and Lord of Lords. He will receive your report and subsequently present it to your heavenly Father."

You are humbled and honored beyond comprehension. Two questions form in your mind. What is the highest expression of loving obedience that I can report to our heavenly Father? The second, is there any higher expression of loving obedience from the body of Christ in America than to present to him the United States, a discipled nation?

Your cup runneth over. In the year 2025, with joy and anticipation, you are prepared and able to present to our heavenly Father, the United States, a discipled nation.

Here is how it can happen . . .

"Therefore, go and make disciples of all nations, baptizing them in the name of the Father and of the Son and of the Holy Spirit, and teaching them to obey everything I have commanded you." (Matthew 28:19–20).

CHAPTER 1

Discovered . . .
A Proclamation Victory

THE REALIZATION DID not come to me all at once. It grew over a period of years, first from personal observations and then as the statistical data and polling information continued to build and support the fact. Finally, in June 1990, a Gallup study determined that 74 percent of Americans answer yes to the precise question, "Would you say you have made a commitment to Jesus Christ or not?" Now I was fully convinced, even stunned! It really is true.

Our heavenly Father has given us a magnificent *proclamation victory!* Having studied religious polling data for several years, I knew that 89 percent of Americans perceive themselves as Christians and that even today the 1993–94 volume of the Barna Report series, speaking of adult Americans, affirms that, "85 percent believe that Jesus was crucified, died, and was resurrected and *is spiritually alive today.*" How curious that the discovery of such widespread belief in the living Christ, his resurrection, and the confession of his spiritual existence is not recognized by Christians for what it truly is: a magnificent proclamation victory of monumental significance! How strange that the presence and importance of this spiritual phenomenon remains unseen, unrecognized, and its potential undefined and unacted upon by the Christian church in the United States. With great justification, American Christians may ask the question, "Does there exist today any nation where, since its very beginning, Christians have more diligently, more fervently, more obediently, more perseveringly shared the Good News of Jesus Christ than in the United States?" The question can be further enlarged to include those related to carrying the message to other nations in the farthest corners of the world. The answer to those questions enables us to possess and act upon the promise in Colossians 3:23–24, "Whatever you do, work at it with all your heart, as working for the Lord, not for men, since you know that you will receive an inheritance from the Lord as a reward. It is the Lord you are serving." God has graciously kept his promise, and we have this magnificent proclamation victory as our rightful inheritance!

A compelling statement of proclamation victory is made by the presence of more than 350,000 Christian churches in the United States. We have more churches per capita than any other nation in the world. This national presence is strengthened by the diversity of 164 Christian denominations, twenty-five of which have more than one million members. Proclamation success flows from two contrasting strengths in American Christianity: unity and diversity. A powerful national unity of faith is revealed in the statistical determination that 85 percent of Americans believe in the divine attributes and spiritual existence of Jesus Christ. Proclamation effectiveness is further empowered by the diversity of spiritual gifts and proclamation methods and strategies employed by churches.

In addition to the millions of believers who are members of churches, millions readily confess faith in Jesus Christ but do not attend nor hold membership in any church.

THE STRENGTH OF PARACHURCH MINISTRIES

Alongside the church, numerous parachurch ministries are working to spread the gospel. Campus Crusade for Christ in 1991 had more than 18,000 students involved in 400 Crusade chapter ministries across the nation. InterVarsity, Focus on the Family, Christian Business Men's Committee, Teen-Challenge, and hundreds of others are all successfully engaged in sharing the Good News.

The diversity of audiences reached by this massive array of Christian organizations engaged in witnessing obedience is mind-challenging. Consider the unique effort of Christian Business Men's Committee. Although international in scope, its major work is performed in the United States. Founded by men of vision who understood the times, members of CBMC present what are called outreach lunches and dinners weekly and monthly. Speakers are always other businessmen, skilled in describing the excitement and satisfaction in their lives since they met Jesus Christ. This is done by carefully describing religious issues and experiences in secular English, totally devoid of Christian jargon. The idea is for members to bring business guests who have not yet committed their lives to Jesus Christ. The goal is to have a lunch or dinner where at least fifty percent of those in attendance are uncommitted businessmen. Speakers are carefully briefed. They are not to preach, present a devotional, or bemoan the sin in the world. Their assignment is to describe their life before they came to know Jesus Christ, to tell how they came to know him, and then relate the changes that have come into their lives since their personal relationship with him began. Members of CBMC understand that while every soul is equally precious in the eyes of the Lord, there are strategic souls, the winning of whom influences the winning of many more.

At the opposite end of the cultural spectrum exists a work of such loving obedience, such humble compassion, such quiet endurance, that its important contribution to our proclamation victory goes largely unnoticed. I speak of what God must consider one of his great treasures on earth, that oasis of loving-kindness serving the inner cities of America known as the city rescue mission. Christians discovered the homeless many generations ago. Long before it became another media charity fad to be supported by other people's money through the coercive power of taxation, the local churches were already there. They had been giving their time, their love, their serving presence, their financial resources for many decades.

In Lansing, Michigan, during 1992, the mission served more than 65,000 meals and provided overnight lodging for more than 9000 men, women, and children. Chapel service attendance totaled 63,154 during the year. The Good News was preached to the poor.

We are to preach the Good News to the poor, as directed by Jesus. When the messenger from John the Baptist came to Jesus, asking, "Are you the one who was to come, or should we expect someone else?" Jesus replied, "Go back and report to John what you have seen and heard: The blind receive sight, the lame walk, those who have leprosy are cured, the deaf hear, the dead are raised, and the good news is preached to the poor" Christians today, who in lovingkindness serve and preach the Good News to the poor, are living examples of Jesus and are positioned at the forefront of those who have achieved the proclamation victory.

CHRISTIANS ARE ALL AROUND US

Perhaps most important of all are the day-to-day personal experiences in my own life that establish the presence and reach of proclamation victory. As an example, after I had gotten gasoline, the gas station attendant who, waiting for me to sign the charge slip, noticed a Charles Stanley tape on the car seat beside me and said, "I watch him on TV. He's good." Thus began a new friendship as I loaned him the tape and many other discipling aids over the weeks and months following.

My wife, Phyllis, and I have Saturday breakfast weekly at a small neighborhood restaurant. As we stood by the cash register to pay our check one Saturday, a young black cook came by and said softly, "I watched you pray before you eat. That's cool." We knew we were brothers in Christ. Another time in another restaurant, shortly after we had placed our order, another couple sat down at the table next to Phyllis and me. We were seated in a row of tables for two with only six inches or so of space between them. We spoke softly so as not to impose our conversation on the patrons seated so close to us. I began to think ahead to the time when our meal would be served, and it came time to thank God and ask his blessing on our food. I noticed that even the most softly expressed prayer would encompass the couple seated next to us. My faith persuades me, and Scripture admonishes that a Christian must never be ashamed of Jesus Christ. The couple beside us proved they also held the same conviction, because they were served first and as the waitress left their table, they bowed their heads, and he softly and reverently thanked the Lord and asked his blessing on their meal.

I received a note from a prominent local businessman after I had presented my Christian perspective on a moral issue in a letter to the editor of our local paper. In it, he thanked me and added, "You wrote what I wanted to say." How promising that Christians are encouraged to speak up in response to even the most humble expression of faith. The anecdotal evidence is too strong to be ignored.

On the basis of historical continuity, scriptural affirmation, a pervasive Christian national presence, statistically and experientially, the evidence is overwhelming. Our heavenly Father has given us a magnificent proclamation victory!

RELIGION OR SPORTS—WHICH ONE WINS?

One of the prevailing myths is that Americans have a greater interest in sports than in religion. Considering media budgets of space, time, and staff devoted to sports, one would think of sports as being far more popular with the public than religion. Not so, according to the late George Cornell, preeminent religion writer and editor for the Associated Press for twenty-seven years.

In the final column of his long and distinguished career, just prior to his retirement, George Cornell fired a major salvo at the disparity between the high interest in religion by millions of Americans and the meager attention it receives in the news media. Using a comparative analysis of interest level based upon individual participation and financial commitment, Mr. Cornell presented convincing evidence that Americans have far greater interest in religion than in sports.

Zeroing in on this compelling issue, Mr. Cornell made these points. "Newly gathered comparative statistics in the 1990s on two key yardsticks of human interest—financial and personal involvement—show religion to be ahead of sports. Yet religion gets only a tiny fraction of media notice compared with the huge volume of attention lavished on sports.

"The latest comparative figures collected on religion and sports find that money contributed to religion totaled $56.7 billion in 1992, according to the American Association of Fund Raising Council. That is about fourteen times the $4 billion spent on the three biggest sports, major league baseball, football, and basketball."

Moving into the equally impressive analysis of personal involvement measured by attendance, Mr. Cornell continued,

"The latest tally of overall attendance at all United States sporting events, gathered in 1990 by the Daily Racing Form, totaled 388 million, including both professional and college football, baseball, basketball, hockey, boxing, tennis, soccer, wrestling, harness, automobile and dog racing.

"By comparison, religious attendance of 5.2 billion in 1990 was about thirteen times the overall sports total. More people turned out for worship in one month—about 433 million—than the 388 million total all year at all the sporting events combined."

Cornell made the point that similar studies since 1973 had the, "same striking contrasts as today. Religion far exceeds sports in attracting people's time and money." These statistics are another persuasive building block supporting the conclusion that our heavenly Father has given United States Christians a magnificent proclamation victory.

CHRISTIAN SCHOOLS ON THE RISE

Evidence of proclamation victory takes many forms and reflects varied degrees of conviction and understanding. One example of deep conviction exists in the dramatic increase in Christian schools, resulting from Supreme Court removal of prayer and the court's suppression of moral and religious values taught in all local public schools.

Resilience has been a hallmark of Christian character over centuries of persecution, oppression, mistreatment, and government intrusion. But rarely in the twentieth century has this quality of the flexible tenacity of American Christians been more tested than in their response to the Supreme Court's astonishing assault on the core values that have dominated the learning atmosphere of all previous generations of American school children.

Pursuing a secular mind-set, seemingly oblivious to and ignorant of the Christian spirit influencing the framers of the

Constitution, whose desire was to protect the people's freedom to worship however they chose without fear of government interference, the Supreme Court presses its attack upon religious freedom across the nation. In 1963, prayer was removed from the public schools. At that time, fewer than 1000 Christian schools existed in the United States. Unsung and unnoticed, it also marked the beginning of a quiet rebellion by Christian parents in the development of their own private school systems, and the beginning of a massive shift to home schooling.

Terence McLean, award winning columnist and broadcaster, in an article titled "America's Best-Kept Secret," wrote, "Christian moms and dads did not take to the streets, they did not burn flags, and while secular history sees the court decision as a yawner, in fact, a revolution began. It is a revolution that is not over yet."

In his remarkable chronology of the United States Supreme Court's assault on religious values beginning in 1963, McLean correlates the accelerated growth of Christian schools as parents accepted the personal and financial sacrifice required to remove their children from a public school system in severe moral and scholastic decline.

Writing in the *Beavercreek News-Current*, Beavercreek, Ohio, Mr. McLean reported: "By 1970 there were approximately 2,600 Christian schools. As a result of *Ohio v. Whisner*, it became unconstitutional for a Board of Education to refer to or use God in any of its official writings. That happened in 1976, and by then there were over 5000 Christian schools.

Since then, in a subsequent series of decisions unparalleled in history, the Supreme Court gutted the public school system of any form of biblical display, biblical reference, and biblical teaching. Invocations, prayers, and benedictions were banned, resulting in Christian parents' accelerating their children's exodus from an increasingly values-neutral learning and social environment. According to the listing published by the Library of

Congress, today more than 32,000 Christian schools are operating in America.

Although student attendance at Christian schools is lower than at public schools, quite astonishing is that today, thirty-one years after the Supreme Court stripped prayer from the public schools, more than one of every four, or 27 percent, of secondary and elementary schools in the United States are Christian schools. And across the nation hundreds of thousands of home-schoolers add to the significance of what McLean calls "America's best-kept secret."

Lawmakers, educators, and parents should recognize that along with the diminishing presence of those children whose parents' deep convictions led to their removal from the public schools, teen pregnancies, violence and classroom chaos increased and SAT scores tumbled.

The correlation among the banning of prayer, declining Christian presence, elimination of any hint of religious symbol or expression and the increased evil of violence and disorder along with a measurably reduced learning experience should hold some lesson for us. After all, one plus one still equals two. And two minus two still equals zero.

EVEN THE YOUTH ARE CONVINCED

Any claim for a proclamation victory would be seriously weakened without strong support for its existence among the youth of our nation. A measure of such proof was provided when more than 170,000 young people converged on Denver in August 1993 to see and hear Pope John Paul II. Here was a marvelous opportunity for the national media to provide their audiences with the real news of the event. Young people by the thousands gathered for the purpose of learning truths about the meaning of life, truth as learned and taught by a world-renowned Christian leader, a person who is, as anyone who has read the encyclical letter, *The Splendor of Truth*, knows, a biblical scholar of profound wisdom. The pope is a twentieth-century leader whose contribution to the collapse of communism will be recognized as long as history is honorably taught. However, the national media once again revealed its weakness in the dimension of spiritual character and were unable to capture the essence of the moment, and missed the story. One person, however, understood. Syndicated columnist, Cal Thomas, reported as follows: "The pope correctly diagnosed America's problem after the victory over Soviet communism. It is moral exhaustion and an inability to distinguish right from wrong. 'All the great causes that are yours today will have meaning only to the extent that you guarantee the right to life and protect the human person,' said the pope in a not-so-veiled reference to America's thirty million abortions in the past twenty years.

"Paraphrasing the Old Testament prophet Isaiah, the pope said, 'Let us pause and reason together,' adding, 'To educate without a value system based on truth is to abandon young people to moral confusion, personal insecurity and easy manipulation. No country, not even the most powerful, can endure if it deprives its own children of this essential good.'

"Now there was a statement worthy of discussion and comment—but the press mostly ignored it." Cal Thomas obviously marches to a different drummer. He closed his column with this observation: "Still, 170,000 young people is pretty impressive, particularly when you consider that the Christ of whom the pope spoke changed the world by starting with only twelve."

A SKEPTIC CONVINCED

The idea of a national proclamation victory is not readily subscribed to without credible evidence or some convincing personal experience. A close friend described his skepticism and the subsequent events that finally led to his recognition and understanding that God has truly blessed American Christians with a wonderful proclamation victory. He told of a young friend who, upon returning from a Promise Keepers' regional meeting, was decidedly and noticeably different. The light in his eyes held a new sense of purpose and meaning. An aura of inner peace and direction existed where before there was uncertainty and aimlessness. They had lunch, and my friend asked him what was happening that was so good in his life. This was his story.

As an adolescent at Sunday school, he remembered being deeply moved by the story of Jesus. He sensed the meaning of Jesus' love in his suffering and death in acceptance of the punishment we deserved for our sins. The boy's heart was tender, and he confessed his sins and gratefully accepted Jesus as his resurrected Savior. His family was not a church-going family and when he excitedly told them what had happened, the joy of his experience was met with indifference and apathy. Months turned into years, and instead of becoming an obedient, discipling Christian he became an unfruitful, undiscipled believer. He joined the ranks of millions who have met Jesus Christ through the remarkably effective and faithfully pursued evangelical process only to be forgotten, left undiscipled, unmentored, ineffective, spiritually alone, and unfruitful in a hostile culture. After twenty years, the Holy Spirit drew him to Promise Keepers, where the light of his life was re-ignited and he renewed his commitment to Jesus Christ. My friend invited him to become his discipling protégé, and they have been meeting regularly since.

As our good friend finished his story, he said, "I have known this young man for several years and had no idea he was a Christian. I realize now there are millions like him who have been reached by the evangelical effectiveness and fervor of the Christian community, but because of a lack of vision, mission and strategy are left to disciple themselves. I am now convinced we truly have a stupendous proclamation victory in the United States."

THE TIME FOR ACTION IS NOW

In 1 Chronicles 12, thousands of leaders from each of the twelve tribes come to David at Hebron to turn Saul's kingdom over to him as the Lord had instructed them. They are described as men armed for battle, brave warriors, loyal, experienced soldiers. However, the contribution from one tribe is strikingly different. There are only 200 men from the tribe of Issachar. Furthermore, they are not warriors, but they are received with dignity and obvious respect. The people of God know that these are men of wisdom. Their character is defined in 1 Chronicles 12:32 as "men of Issachar, who understood the times and knew what Israel should do." *Who understood the times and knew what Israel should do.* Knowing and doing are inseparable elements in the pursuit and accomplishment of worthy goals. Knowledge by itself is passive and ineffective. Action driven by vain ambition without sufficient knowledge will invariably be unproductive and even destructive. Desired results, then, are produced only in a marriage of appropriate knowledge with organized action.

God has favored our nation above all others with a twentieth-century proclamation victory of unparalleled magnitude. The potential for discipleship is indefinable and requires, first of all, our fervent prayer that he will bring forth leaders possessing biblical wisdom, men and women who understand the times and know what Christians should do, and Christlike examples, who will teach their fellow servants in Christ how to know and do what is right.

Our source of wisdom is Jesus Christ. The road to wisdom is God's Word. John, the disciple especially loved by Jesus, brought these truths together in John 1:1–2, "In the beginning was the Word, and the Word was with God, and the Word was God. He was with God in the beginning." Jesus further establishes a fundamental truth that he, the Word, and Wisdom are one when in John 8:31–32 (NRS) Jesus declares, "If you continue in my word, you are truly my disciples. Then you will know the truth, and the truth will make you free." In the magnificent proclamation victory God has so graciously given us, there exists for Christians the glorious hope that, early in the twenty-first century, they can proclaim to the world, "Blessed is our nation whose God is the Lord!"

This will not come to pass, however, unless each Christian personally develops three qualities of Christian character essential to the discipling of our nation: faith, obedience, and love.

The time has arrived for Christians to ask themselves deep, penetrating, and soul-searching questions. Here are a few:

How is it possible that a proclamation triumph of such magnitude and national significance remains unknown to and undefined by the media and, more important, to the body of Christ in America today?

When will we mobilize the spiritual and material resources of the 350,000 churches in the United States to undertake the discipling now called for and, in fact, commanded by God's Word?

What spiritual weakness has caused this blindness?

Where is the leadership of laity and clergy calling for Great Commission obedience and follow-through?

Is there a universal, unconfessed sin draining spiritual power, discernment, and effectiveness from the body of Christ? The answer, of course, is yes!

Why have we failed to proclaim this victory for Christ?

How have we arrived at this level of skepticism and this incredible state of indifference?

Where is the biblical analysis and exposure of the brilliant successes of Satan, whose existence is clearly outlined in the

Bible? We treat him as a joke, masquerading in the minds of those in cultural surrender as a comical figure in red tights, with a long tail, and carrying a pitchfork. He is the one who replaces our courage with a lust for conformity and leads our shameful retreat into cultural and psychological isolation. He is the one who masterminds with strategic brilliance, dissension, and factions within local churches and replaces the creative energies of Christ's love with the selfish pursuit of vain personal agenda.

What strategic paradigm shifts are required to bring Christian thinking and actions into obedient harmony with the Great Commission vision of Jesus Christ?

And finally, one of the most demanding questions of our time. How is it possible for this widespread belief to exist while our nation continues an accelerating decline into moral degeneracy?

It is our prayerful intention to answer these questions and many others in the pages ahead.

CHAPTER 2

Uncovered . . . A Great Commission Failure

ELTON TRUEBLOOD WROTE, "The test of the vitality of a religion can be seen in its impact on culture." The hard truth of that statement is so relative to the accelerating degeneracy of moral climate in our nation that, as a Christian, its validity causes me to squirm uncomfortably. With the continued softening of Christian character, we should consider the viability of Mr. Trueblood's statement reversed and paraphrased. The measure of the decadence of American culture can be seen in its impact on Christian character.

We closed the first chapter with what many consider one of the most demanding and perplexing questions of our time: How is it that with so many people believing in Jesus our culture continues to decline morally? It springs from the broad scope of religious belief existing simultaneously with an accelerating moral decline.

The answer is this (and, Christian, prayerfully ponder this answer from the deep recesses of your soul): Our heavenly Father has given us a magnificent proclamation victory, but we have responded with a monumental discipling failure!

We have all this belief, but it is passive, undiscipled, disobedient, ineffective belief. Instead of following up this magnificent proclamation victory with discipling obedience, we have been distracted and diverted from our central purpose, which is to make disciples by teaching obedience to everything Jesus has commanded us. We have surrendered to the attractions of a materialistic and degenerate culture. While many Christians have been engaged in proclamation, we have been disengaged in discipling. Discipling is the obedient, prayerful, more difficult, follow-up work of transforming the spiritual infancy of the newly committed, the biblically illiterate, lambs of God into obedient, spirit-filled, mature disciples of Jesus Christ.

Discipling is both easier and more difficult than proclaiming. Communication between two people is enhanced in a discipling relationship because of the common ground of belief in Jesus Christ and the presence of the Holy Spirit existing in both believers. Proclamation can frequently be accomplished at arm's length, while teaching obedience requires disciplined study and prayerful sensitivity in a mentoring, tutoring relationship. Discipling becomes a sacrificial investment of time and love in the lives of others. Discipling responsibility begins at home, with the family. Surely, a sound biblical premise is that a person who willfully confesses belief in the life, death, and resurrection of Jesus Christ cannot do so without Holy Spirit intervention. That person will be spiritually responsive to the loving discipling of someone who cares, especially someone who wants to be a teaching friend and guide the believer into biblical truths leading to a life dominated by the spiritual qualities of love, joy, peace, patience, kindness, goodness, faithfulness, gentleness, and self-control.

NEVER BECOME DISTRACTED FROM YOUR CENTRAL PURPOSE

Among the 23,000 publications in the United States, the *Wall Street Journal* is unique. Considered the nation's leading business newspaper with daily circulation approaching two million, its reading audience is large and influential. Recently, its readers were treated to a humorous little poem that went like this.

End Result

> The bumper sticker in my view
>> Was clever, I admit it;
> As soon as I had read it through,
>> I laughed so hard, I hit it.

—DICK EMMONS

As I finished chuckling over this bit of fun verse, I realized there is a profound moral hidden within its humor that may have escaped even the author. The moral is: Never become distracted from your central purpose.

I am an instrument-rated pilot. In aviation, a cardinal rule says that when acting as pilot-in-command of an aircraft in flight, the pilot's central purpose is to fly the airplane. The pilot cannot be distracted by the sudden appearance of a flashing red light on the instrument panel or the rapid-fire instructions from Air Traffic Control. The pilot-in-command must assimilate the information, analyze it accurately, and respond effectively, all the while never becoming diverted from the central purpose, which is to fly the airplane.

What is the central purpose of a Christian life?

Our central purpose is to be an obedient disciple and to make disciples by teaching obedience of all Jesus has commanded. We have not only become distracted by the flashing red lights and rapid-fire sound bytes of the culture; we have also become seduced by, enticed into, and involved in the diversions of the world. Additionally, we have become intimidated by the media into cultural isolation and, in large measure, we have

forgotten and abandoned our central purpose. A major conse-
quence of our discipling failure can be seen in the accelerating
spiritual and moral collapse of our nation. Central-purpose
ignorance and denial afflicts all denominations, all segments of
the body of Christ

HISTORY'S MOST AWESOME TRANSFER OF POWER

For forty days after his resurrection, Jesus moved among his
followers. A major purpose was to establish the amazing reality
that he was truly a risen Savior. He had conquered death. He
was fully alive. His new body was both physical and supernatural. He was the one he claimed to be—the Son of God, Savior
of the world.

A second purpose, almost totally lost on today's Christian,
was to accomplish the transfer of the most awesome power in
the universe, the power embodied in the words of his final
instructions, "All authority in heaven and on earth has been
given to me. Therefore go and make disciples" (Matthew 28:18,
19). Surely these must be among the most important words ever
spoken. They culminate thirty-three years of divine-human life,
including three years of public ministry and forty days as the resurrected Savior. Three sentences echo down the corridors of
time to us today. These are final instructions for future generations. Listen as he presents His mission to you: "All authority in
heaven and on earth has been given to me" (Matthew 28:18–20).
What an astonishing claim! Only one who had proven beyond
all reasonable doubt that he had conquered death, that he was
fully alive, that he was truly a risen Savior, that he was who he
claimed to be, the Son of God, Savior of the world, could possi-
bly make such a claim.

What is the highest, ultimate expression and use of the mind-expanding power residing within us in the person of Jesus Christ? Jesus answers that question clearly and definitively in the majestic commandment of the second sentence of the Great Commission. "Therefore go and make disciples of all nations, baptizing them in the name of the Father and of the Son and of the Holy Spirit, and teaching them to obey everything I have commanded you" (Matthew 28:19), *teaching them to obey everything I have commanded you.* One of the great problems of our time is our failure as Christians to understand the piercing truth and eternal implications in this extension of ultimate authority from Jesus to all humanity. The obedient act of making a disciple is the ultimate expression and use of all authority in heaven and on earth. This must forever be the central purpose of a Christian's life, because through this divine process, *you and I are empowered to replicate Jesus Christ in the life of another person. The replication of Jesus in the life of another is the intended use of all authority in heaven and on earth.*

Our Lord's mandate requires every Christian to participate in the discipling of our nation. Discipling obedience begins at home in the immediate family. Then we need to disciple friends, neighbors, and coworkers in need of biblical mentoring who are identified by the Holy Spirit through our prayers. It is not, repeat, not necessary for the Christian to possess perfect understanding before teaching obedience to another. Since we will never have complete knowledge and should always be learning biblical truth, the time to begin discipling is today. Compassion and love for others form the basic foundation. These spiritual qualities are formed in our heart as we pray for the one to be taught. If these truths of Great Commission obedience were understood and acted upon by Christians today, early in the twenty-first century, Christians in the United States could proclaim to the world, "Blessed is our nation whose God is the Lord!"

WHY DON'T WE DISCIPLE?

Our discipling failure results from absence of biblical vision, ignorance of biblical mission, and biblical illiteracy relating to the strategic work of the Holy Spirit in the local church. And, of course, a major problem is the naiveté of the entire church toward Satan's strategy for victory. These problems are not exclusive to any denomination or theologically affiliated groups of denominations. These weaknesses of spiritual character dominate all 164 Christian denominations in the United States. From mainline to evangelical, from Roman Catholic to Pentecostal, the need to focus on Jesus Christ and his discipling example is the unrecognized and tragic failure of American Christianity during the second half of the twentieth century.

We Are Skeptical

Instead of faith, the Christian psyche today is dominated by skepticism. I have the privilege of speaking at Christian writer conferences across the nation as well as at churches, college journalism, and college communication-arts classes. After presenting the statistical evidence for the broad base of religious belief and Christian presence existing in the United States, the questions of doubt and skepticism invariably come. Instead of rejoicing in faith and immediately searching for abounding opportunities to disciple, the glorious news of proclamation victory is rejected in the subtle sin of skepticism and cynicism. The responses invariably become, "Yes, but ...," "Yes, but ...," "Yes, but ..." What is the character of this belief? What is the depth of this belief? What is the commitment of this belief? What is the understanding of this belief? The answer to these questions is exactly what you would expect in an undiscipled nation. It is all of the following and more—this belief is shallow, weak, uncertain, indifferent, confused, filled with misconceptions, wavering, anxious, tentative, fearful, lonely, rebellious, truculent, defensive, ashamed, filled with the guilt of unconfessed sin, bitter, and disappointed in an agony of regret and remorse over broken relationships and unkept promises, both given and received.

We Are Insensitive

Further, believers are biblically illiterate, unmentored, untutored, and undiscipled. It is what it is because or our discipling failure—yours and mine. *Whatever the gap or difference between where believers' faith is and where you believe it should be biblically, the difference is our discipling responsibility, yours and mine!* We have neglected the Great Commission.

On the west side of Lansing on a little-used side street is a small church named Bretton Woods Covenant Church. We have been members for thirty-five years or so. It is part of a national denomination called the Evangelical Covenant Church of America. Perhaps it should be called the Discipling Covenant Church of America, a name, while not descriptive of its sense of mission, would be more in tune with the challenge of the times. Our church is a microcosmic example of thousands of churches across our nation. In conversations with the majority of the men from the church, the name of Jesus Christ is rarely, if ever, mentioned. Discipling is not discussed. Problems of sin and the joy of spiritual victory through repentance and confession give way to golf scores and favored football teams. These are good people. I love them. They, too, deplore the deteriorating moral climate in our nation

What we don't realize is that all believers are family! These 85 percent who believe in Jesus are spiritual infants in the pews around us! These babes in Christ work beside us at the office and in the factory. These are lambs of God. These are the lambs of whom Jesus spoke when He said to Peter, "Peter do you really love me?" Peter said, "Yes Lord, You know that I love You." Jesus said, "Feed my lambs." We should be heartbroken and weeping over these lambs of God, these babes in Christ, these spiritual infants, whom we have abandoned on the doorstep of the world. They make up the majority of every denomination. Has there been any time in history when the words of Jesus spoke more clearly to his followers than they speak to Christians in America today? "I tell you, open your eyes and look at the fields! They are ripe for harvest" (John 4:35).

We are guilty of the neglect, abuse, and abandonment of these children of God. America is a nation whose soul is crying out for discipling. We have been presented with a discipling harvest field that is historically unprecedented. How it must grieve our heavenly Father to see our lack of vision and our insensitivity.

The following true experience serves as a classic example of the discipling insensitivity of the church at large. She had been hurt and abused as a child. There was a divorce and rejection by both her mother and father. Uncaring foster homes left additional wounds and scars. Even as a young adult, at times she seemed like a small child who only wanted to climb on someone's lap and be hugged and loved. Yet there was no bitterness, no meanness of spirit. There was, however, a quiet inner desperation to find the quality of love she had never experienced but somehow knew existed. In the deep longing of her soul she understood that somewhere, in someone, she would find unconditional love.

Most of her close friends shared similar backgrounds of broken homes, fractured families. All had lived through a child's greatest fear of losing one or both of their parents. Then one of her friends had the idea of studying the Bible. Since none attended church, they began an unstructured, unled, regular

Bible study. They read aloud and discussed the meaning of the words. Because they were yielded and open, the Holy Spirit led them into the understanding of truth. She met Jesus Christ and surrendered her heart and life to him. He fulfilled her lifelong spiritual and emotional search with the highest, purest form of unconditional love.

She joined a church to participate in the friendship of others who had likewise surrendered their lives to him. One month after joining the church, the pastor's wife said to her, "Of course, now that you're a member of the church, you'll want to start wearing dresses instead of those pantsuits, won't you?" Instead of seeing the heartfelt, discipling need of this spiritual infant, this babe in Christ, this lamb of God, the pastor's wife was engulfed in the subtle sin of the vanity of cultural conformity. Whether it be the church's culture or the world's culture, how tragic to assign them a higher priority than discipling in love. She now attends a church where discipling in lovingkindness and a forgiving spirit, both conditions of the heart, are more important than what others wear.

We Are Biblically Illiterate

Biblical illiteracy must be recognized as one of the major reasons for our discipling failure. When polls show that fewer than 17 percent of Americans read the Bible regularly, we realize the massive state of disobedience in which Christians are willing to live. Jesus said, "If you continue in my word, you are truly my disciples; and you will know the truth, and truth will make you free" (John 8:31–32 RSV). Effective discipling begins with obedience. We are to obey by staying in the Word. One of the great sorrows of our time and another that must grieve the heart of our heavenly Father is the failure of Christians to inspire by example and communication a hunger, a thirst, a love, for the infallible truth of his holy Word.

Biblical illiteracy spawns serious weaknesses in Christian character. Hosea 4:6 states, "My people are destroyed from a lack of knowledge." Lack of knowledge leaves Christians today without any sense of biblical vision, mission, or strategy. They remain ignorant of the central purpose of discipling that brings Christ-centered meaning and power into their lives.

A MONUMENTAL DISCIPLING FAILURE

Evidence of our discipling failure is everywhere around us. Where once our nation was internationally recognized for its moral and spiritual leadership, tragically, we now lead the world in the most degenerate areas of shameful and immoral behavior. Our nation has become number one in divorce, teen pregnancy, and violent crime. With less than 5 percent of the world's population, we consume over 50 percent of the world's supply of cocaine. We lead all nations in drug use and follow closely in the number of abortions. The United States is considered the pornography capital of the world. We also lead in single-parent homes and teen suicide. No longer can there be any question that we are in a moral crisis of unprecedented proportion. Our nation today is mired in the consequences of a monumental discipling failure by those whom God holds accountable for its spiritual character: Christians!

Has proclamation succumbed to the subtle sin of the vanity of just getting large numbers of believers, largely ignoring the Great Commission discipling mandate of Jesus? Has the time long passed when a massive transition of resource investment from proclamation to discipling should have taken place? Does the biblical wisdom of understanding the times and knowing what Christians should do require us to begin a new era of discipling our nation by building on the proclamation victory God has so graciously given us? Surely this would be a paradigm shift biblically appropriate to the dawn of the twenty-first century!

On my desk at this moment is a religious news brief highlighting an appeal from a major denomination to one of the nation's foremost Christians. He is being urged to bring together leaders from every denomination and parachurch group for the purpose of developing a strategy to present the gospel to every American by the year 2000. I cannot imagine a more disastrous miscalculation in the stewardship of Great Commission resources relating to spiritual energy, time, and money, not to mention the confusion such undiscerning effort will cause in the minds of their followers as it becomes evident they are engaged in the fruitless pursuit of a victory already achieved. Certainly a far more timely and fruitful purpose would be to organize a massive Christian effort to disciple our nation: a total mobilization of all Christians and their spiritual and material resources to disciple our nation. Now, there, is a biblical goal worthy of such a gathering!

FRONT-LINE COMBATANTS IN A SPIRITUAL WAR

What prevents Christian leaders from hearing what the pollsters are saying? For 300 years we have prayed for Americans to receive and believe the Good News. God has heard our prayers and has answered them. The evidence is in and it's overwhelming. Americans believe the gospel. Now, instead of escalating proclamation, which is 85 percent accomplished, we have to teach obedience to make the United States a discipled nation. This requires a totally new paradigm shift.

Christians continually fail to understand they are front-line combatants in a spiritual war for the hearts, minds, and souls of the American people. In all-out war, if one side steadfastly refuses to acknowledge its participation in the conflict or even the existence of a war, it will be blind to the deceptive strategies of the enemy, Satan. Who else could be responsible for a deception of such scope and magnitude where 150 million members of 164 denominations continue to pour spiritual energy, time, money, and faith into the pursuit of a proclamation victory already achieved? Satan's influence can be seen in our culture. Such a satanic victory can only be implemented and sustained in a spiritual vacuum created by the absence of Christian righteousness and a pervasive ignorance of biblical truth. Both conditions are engendered by the biblical illiteracy of a nation where less than 17 percent of the people read the Bible regularly and where an estimated 95 percent of evangelicals would fail to pass a biblical literacy test.

In the annals of spiritual warfare, our national discipling failure may actually be Satan's greatest undercover victory of all time, a covert operation so successful in the continued, unrecognized diversion of strategic discipling resources that it would relegate major CIA and KGB subversive successes to the status of kindergarten exercises.

THE REWARDS OF DISCIPLING

As the incoming president of the National Business Forms Association, I was required to give a twenty-minute speech at our annual convention. The message was to set the tone, establish the theme, identify the challenges, and define the goals for my one-year term as president. The banquet setting was the main ballroom of the Hyatt Regency in downtown Atlanta. More than 1,400 corporation presidents, owners, and spouses in their elegant attire were being served by white-gloved waiters. It was, by the standards of my humble origins, an impressive affair.

My preparation for this moment had been bathed in prayer. As a secular leader I must be accountable to the responsibility of my office while, at the same time, be identifiably Christian in the culture. Intentionally and by design, my talk was crafted to address both areas. Membership needs of the Association were defined, and solutions to these problems were presented. Spiritual qualities of biblical wisdom leading to good management were reviewed. Unexpectedly, and for the first time at this event, a standing ovation followed. As I stood with Phyllis, my wife, I prayed, "God, please help me handle this." I knew the vanity of human glory is deceptive, addictive, and fleeting.

Sometimes I compare the above experience with my first Sunday school teaching and discipling experience. With barely 100 members, the Bretton Woods Covenant Church in Lansing has been our spiritual fountain for nearly forty years. Long ago, when asked if I would teach the senior high Sunday school class, an instant fear led me to request time to think about it. I had never formally taught anything. I wanted to do it, but I was afraid. These were high school kids. How could I ever relate to them, and they, to me? More important than any other consideration, I knew it was right and that God wanted me to do it. Finally, I agreed.

It was a small group, and I could see the skepticism in their eyes as we gathered for the first time. I opened with prayer and humbled myself before the Lord as I sought his blessing on each one there and asked that we would be a blessing to one another. The study material I had selected dealt with the plight of teens in the inner city. It captured their interest and generated discussion of Christian relevance. Early one Sunday morning while the family slept, I knelt by the sofa and prayed for each of those kids individually by name, and I asked God how I might better serve them. He said, "If you will become smaller and smaller and smaller until you finally disappear, becoming nonexistent, Jesus can go in your place and teach those teens and you will be serving them better." I understood and continued in my prayers that Jesus would be my replacement.

Spring arrived and the Sunday school year drew to a close. By then they were very much at ease, even participating in audible prayer at the end of the hour. It was during such a time of voluntary prayer that one of the teen-age girls, softly and audibly before her peers, prayed, "And thank you Lord for the influence Mr. Russell has been on my life." This treasured moment eclipsed anything else I've ever achieved, and I taught senior-high Sunday school for ten years.

Nothing, absolutely nothing, equals the fulfillment that comes in being an obedient disciple and making disciples of others as Jesus commanded.

CHAPTER 3

Christian Obscurity—
How Did It Happen?

ON THE SURFACE, the idea is preposterous. Its absurdity is nearly indigestible. How can we speak of Christian obscurity in a nation with 150 million church goers attending 350,000 churches with nearly 60 billion dollars of annual giving in a nation where 89 percent of its people perceive themselves as Christians?

With such a significant national presence, a powerful, energetic, dominant Christian influence should exist in all major institutions in the United States. This should be especially true in those institutions holding power to shape, impact, alter, control, or inspire behavioral change. We know that exactly the opposite is true. Secular thinking devoid of biblical influence dominates and controls the direction and output of America's culture-shaping institutions. They include the government, the media, entertainment and the arts, and public education. The erosion and subsequent disappearance of a predominant Christian influence and its replacement by secular control should be a major concern to every Christian. The power of these institutions rests in control of information flow. It exists in the authority to select what kinds of and how much information is disseminated. It lies in delivery style, choice of methods, and channels of distribution. Audiences to be targeted are invariably determined, consciously or subconsciously, by the dominant ideology of the decision makers.

SECULAR THINKING SHAPES OUR CULTURE

In America's vital institutions, power to control information flow is secured through a variety of processes. Such authority may be earned by political election or through bureaucratic survival. It may come through competitive advantage, marketing superiority, entertainment skills, artistic talent, tenure rule, competence rewarded with authority, and countless other methods, any and all of which are available to Christians.

Sadly, Christian presence no longer means a Christian voice or a Christian difference. Astonishingly, most of those in controlling positions are believing Christians. For example, on a recent ABC special on religion, Peter Jennings acknowledged publicly that he attends church. The crucial difference is between believing passively and believing obediently. To be a believing obedient Christian requires discipling courage rising from an inner faith. Such faith is produced through intimacy with Jesus Christ. To know him intimately requires prayerful, regular study of his Word. For what other reason would Jesus say, "If you hold to my teaching, you are really my disciples. Then you will know the truth, and the truth will set you free" (John 8:31–32). Notice the desired result of continuing in his Word is becoming a disciple. It calls for obedience. Obedience is the culture-changing difference. To be a disciple is to be engaged in teaching obedience to truth. It calls for being identifiably Christian in the culture.

By default, Christian obscurity in American institutions has left a devastating impact on national character. Absence of leadership and lack of obedient Christian presence in these critical arenas of idea formation and communication leaves Christians without a national sense of biblical vision, mission, and strategy. Increasingly isolated and with little or no direction on how to participate in meaningful local strategies for achieving the goals of biblical vision and the work of Jesus' discipling mission, Christians retreat further into an enclave of cultural isolation and diminishing moral influence.

Media

Christian obscurity in the news media has subjected the American people to news interpretation by a school of ideological minnows. Philosophical harmony enables them to turn in unison on most any issue as they apply their ideological censorship through a well-honed technique of selective emphasis. They have, for the most part, been educated in a world of academic journalism dominated by the philosophy of humanism devoid of biblical influence. From classroom to newsroom, this ideological monopoly of the hard left produces an incestuous monologue of such lock-step secularism as to attract Justice Department investigation if it were any other institution of American life. However, it appears the old nemesis, competition, in the form of alternative news sources will soon end the stranglehold of this tired, out-of-touch, intellectually bankrupt monopoly.

Study the power of ideological influence on news media managers to select, emphasize, interpret, and shape whatever is presented to its viewing, listening, or reading audience. Surely the field of entertainment and the arts is an example where, under domination of secular influence, the offering has become a product frequently unfit for family enjoyment. Loss of information control to secular thought was caused over time by the voiceless shell of hollowed-out believers. Strength of existing biblical conviction and courage was replaced by the emptiness of television laziness, the sensual attractions of modern entertainment, and the pursuit of meaningless pastimes in a world of mounting leisure. Biblical illiteracy prevailed, and all sense of kingdom vision, mission, and strategy was lost. Instead of providing Christlike examples, leaders became trend followers and pursued vain personal agenda. Pronouncement retreated to the religious ghetto of the Saturday morning religion page, and Christian publishers passively accepted banishment of their literary successes from deserved recognition on national best-seller lists. Christian obscurity accelerated as comfort zones of conformity replaced the intentional purpose of discipling obedience. Media intimidation gradually herded Christian expression into cultural isolation. While the voice of Christian discipling grew faint almost to extinction, the outside world moved into and began to dominate the living rooms and lives of Christians through television news and entertainment. As the age of electronic communication flourished, the astonishing and shameful surrender of Christian witness in all aspects of American culture continued. Those possessing the authority of Jesus Christ, who are commanded by their King to make disciples of all nations, instead submitted their families, their culture, and their nation to the virtually unopposed influence of the forces of evil that will always occupy any vacuum caused by spiritual shallowness, shame, and fear. The authority of God's truth was lost to them. Christians did not speak out against evil invading the land. They became afraid to use the spiritual power within them. "For God did not give us a spirit of timidity, but a spirit of power, of love and of self-discipline" (2 Timothy 1:7).

Government

Consider the binding impact of regulation imposed on our lives by the three branches of government—executive, legislative, and judicial.

Christian obscurity in government has cost the American people the untold blessing of taking the leadership and responsibility in the great cause of caring for the poor, the wayward, and the helpless of our nation. Christians have denied themselves the blessing promised in, "Give, and it will be given to you." Christians aren't taking their responsibility in taking care of those who are less fortunate.

Education

By almost any measure of learning quality or end-result standards, had survival of our educational system been subjected to the competitive forces of a free-market environment, our system of public education would have collapsed and been replaced many years ago. Christian obscurity in education, especially on the local school board, has left interpretation of court rulings to the distorted view and ambition of those on the academic left. School administrators, unsupported by alternative views, are led to implement antireligious judicial mandates far beyond their legal scope, intention, and permissibility. Sadly, this takes place even though these administrators and board members are Christian.

Entertainment and the Arts

Christian obscurity in the field of entertainment and the arts has created a wasteland of inspiration described in *World* magazine by Carl F. H. Henry as follows: "The profanity that now invades television screens and some newspapers should be challenged. This normality may reflect the routine dinner-table conversation of some network executives, producers, and actors, though I doubt it. It represents more than poverty of speech. The names of God and of Christ are blatantly misused by those who are religiously stupid—they no longer associate those terms with spiritual reality. But the air waves are not the private property of the uncivilized."

THE CYCLE OF CHARACTER TRANSFORMATION

Christian obscurity—how did it happen? In a study of the rise and fall of great nations and civilizations, an early American, Professor Alexander Tyler, identified a cycle of character transformation experienced by the people of extraordinary societies. He determined that people of great nations invariably followed a behavioral transformation in which they moved: From *bondage* to *spiritual faith*; from *spiritual faith* to *great courage*; from *great courage* to *abundance*; from *abundance* to *selfishness*; from selfishness to *complacency*; from *complacency* to *apathy*; from apathy to *dependency*; from *dependency* back into b*ondage* again.

Because our nation has experienced a major social and economic restructuring during the 300 years since Tyler's study, some updating and refinement of his captivating transformation cycle seems in order. A modern view of the historical cycle of character transformation in people of great nations and civilizations would be as follows: People go from *bondage* or *severe persecution* to *spiritual faith*; from *spiritual faith* to *courage*; from *courage* to *liberty*; from *liberty* to *abundance*; from a*bundance* to *selfishness*; from *selfishness* to *dependency*; from *dependency* to *degeneracy*; and from *degeneracy* back into *bondage* again..

The conclusion of this cycle is not inevitable. In both biblical and modern history, there have been those nations in which an obedient remnant has come forth with great commitment, conviction, and understanding of the times to lead a spiritual regeneration and national discipling from which, once again, national character was restored to the liberating strengths of spiritual faith and courage.

The compelling progression of this behavioral cycle rings with such truth that most Americans respond with the obvious question, "Where are we in relation to that cycle?" Where is the United States in this cycle? What have we become as a people?

When the emphasis of a people is focused on spiritual qualities in the ascending phases of the cycle, the national character is dominated by faith and courage, unselfishness, compassion for others, moral fidelity, and freedom from bondage. Most Americans see the United States on the descending or negative side. To me, there is strong evidence that, as a people, we are experiencing with increasing intensity all four conditions defined on the negative side. In varying degrees, we can define a national presence of selfishness, dependency, degeneracy, and bondage.

Selfishness

No person in the world is without something to give. Spiritual possessions (love, compassion, tenderness, thankfulness, faithfulness, forgiveness, joy, and prayer) are more meaningful, precious, and enduring than anything material. In the same realm, gifts without material substance yet sacrificial in time and energy, are comfort, encouragement, a listening ear, and a patient, kindly attitude. Long after the memory of tangible benefits has faded, eternal gifts of the soul are cherished. Surely we can find time to impart these intangible gifts in our busy lives.

The tragic impact of selfishness on American lives is everywhere around us. Elevation of self above the desire for knowledge and obedience to the one who created us leaves sorrow, loneliness, immorality, violence, and fear as the shameful reminder of a nation in historical decline. A poignant excerpt from Dennis Rainey's book, *Lonely Husbands, Lonely Wives*, dramatizes the individual selfishness we have come to accept as a cultural norm. A police officer describes his eye-witness account of the death of a family—a classic example of selfishness, hardness, absence of love and compassion.

There as I watched in disbelief, the husband pointed to the two little girls and said, "Well, which one do you want?" With no apparent emotion, the mother chose the older one. The girls looked at each other; then the older daughter walked out and climbed into the car. The smaller girl, clutching her cabbage patch doll in one hand and her suitcase in the other, watched in bewilderment as her sister and mother drove off. I saw tears streaming down her face. The only "comfort" she received was an order from the father to go into the house, as he turned to talk with some friends. There I stood . . . the unwilling witness to the death of a family.

Sadly, more than 50 percent of marriages today end in divorce. The evil of selfishness drives the break up of the American family. It replaces God's love, his Son, his Word, his Spirit with love of self. It replaces biblical literacy with ignorance of the times and knowledge of what must be done to preserve the blessings of our national spiritual heritage. Vain personal ambitions replace Christian character and obedience with obscurity and discipling impotence. Personal pleasure replaces the self-control of loyalty and faithfulness.

Dependency

Instead of Jesus, Christians today depend on the world. The further we move from Jesus, the more we depend on personal vanity, other people, material possessions, and secular institutions. A degree of our worldly dependence can be seen in the four trillion dollars of debt that Americans have permitted their government to accumulate. In the face of this monstrous obligation, we continue to vote into office those who annually approve and pass budgets adding billions more to this stewardship disaster. We depend on government to do inefficiently, ineffectively, and wastefully what God requires Christians to do in love. We are commanded to provide charity, feed the poor, shelter the homeless, and care for the indigent, the aged, and the sick.

Instead of looking to the truth-revealing power of the Holy Spirit to bring us fulfillment, we depend on secular models, which are inevitably empty and unsatisfying. We seek fulfillment in career advancement, sex, power, control over others, leisure time, vicarious victories through obsession with sports and games, pursuit of vain personal agenda, and the gathering of material possessions. None of these will ever bring the soul-nourishing satisfaction of the fruit of the Spirit defined for us by the apostle Paul: "But the fruit of the Spirit is love, joy, peace, patience, kindness, goodness, faithfulness, gentleness and self-control" (Galatians 5:22).

Degeneracy

In one of Mr. Gorbachev's early visits to the United States, he was questioned about human rights in the Soviet Union. He angrily responded, "What moral right does America have to assume the pose of a teacher? Who has given it the right to teach us moral lessons?" One correspondent reported, "The question is valid and a piercing one that cuts to the heart of what we have become as a people. And the fact that it has not yet been answered is very revealing."

As I review the span of my lifetime, I find it almost incomprehensible to believe any nation, especially one of such previously idealistic and high moral character, could culturally degenerate as rapidly as has the United States. Since 1935 when Americans were shocked to learn the word *damn* was being spoken in a movie conversation to the present, where publicly televised discussions are so primitive, vile, and immoral as to embarrass the vast majority of viewers, obviously we have been overcome by a national moral disaster. A character collapse of such magnitude could happen only in an era of electronic communication, secular control, and Christian timidity. (*Timidity*—a word more kind than accurate.)

Other symptoms of degeneracy abound. One-and-a-half million abortions per year are now being performed in this country. Abortion has become the most common surgical procedure in the nation today. It has been said, "In the U.S., the most dangerous place for a baby to be is in its mother's womb." Teen suicide has increased fourfold since 1962—the year that prayer was removed from the public school system. The most-cited reasons for such youthful despondency are feelings of personal worthlessness and feelings of isolation and loneliness. The greatest fear of a majority of teenagers isn't nuclear war or scholastic failure or poverty—it is losing one or both of their parents. One-half of all children in the United States will be abandoned by their father by the time they are eighteen. Yes, we are an undiscipled nation in the advanced stages of moral degeneracy!

Bondage

If truth is liberating, sin is enslaving. Many years ago I considered myself a social drinker. I enjoyed a glass of wine at home at the end of the day's work, then perhaps another one or two during the evening. Over a period of years, the evening drinks grew to three or four and one day. I realized that late in the afternoon, while still at work, I began looking forward to and thinking about the glass of wine I would have upon my arrival home. I became alarmed because I knew that was a danger signal. A newspaper article suggested if you could go thirty days without drinking, you were not an alcoholic. I was in trouble. Addiction is bondage, and I had permitted myself to become addicted to alcohol. As a youth, I learned I couldn't control the habit of smoking. After I reached two packages a day, I knew I must quit. It wasn't easy. I was in bondage to nicotine. I prayed my way through it after quitting cold. God is faithful.

I had a far more difficult time with alcohol. One evening I attended a meeting of Alcoholics Anonymous. I sensed the presence of faith and the support of fellowship. Though encouraged by the meeting, I still felt I could end the addiction through the power of self-control promised in the definition of the fruit of the Spirit (Galatians 5:22–23). Setting a date thirty days ahead, after which, I resolved never to drink alcohol again, I prayed and went on with my life. The day finally came. If I ever doubted the power of addiction, those doubts were eliminated in the torment of the weeks following. Each desire to yield was met with prayer and the presence and authority of Jesus Christ. Again, as in smoking, the terrible addiction to the bondage of alcohol was broken by spiritual faith and self-control and replaced by the peace and joy of liberty in Jesus Christ.

Fear of violence is another form of *bondage* invading our lives today. Here are some symptoms: Locking our car doors from the inside while we are in them. Driving different routes than we formerly followed. "Call us when you arrive home, so we know you are safe." Number and sophistication of locks on our doors. Electronic alarm systems. Increased training in the arts of self-defense. Training in the use of hand guns as a defensive measure. Continued fear for the safety of our children.

Abnormal and excessive desires of the flesh in any form can be an addictive bondage. Other forms of bondage may be gluttony, laziness, covetousness, power, ambition, vanity, drugs, material possessions, and hundreds of other subtle sins. Christian lives become powerless, lifeless, and dull when they are lived in bondage to cultural conformity. Christians impose upon themselves a terrible bondage in their surrender to the fear of peer and cultural rejection rather than to be be obediently and identifiably Christian in the world. To be identifiably Christian in the culture is to be engaged in discipling directly and by example.

I have come to appreciate the life-changing power existing in the lives of those whose desire is to be obedient rather than

sheltered in conformity, courageous rather than fearful, and
victorious rather than shameful.

OBSCURITY IN THE CHURCH

Christian obscurity in the vital institutions of our culture
has left its most devastating impact on the church itself. A
national directory of publications lists 23,000 publications in the
United States. Some 600 are religious. Over 22,000 are secular.
Ninety-seven percent of all publications in this country are secular. Only 3 percent are religious. One estimate puts fewer than
10 percent of Christians visiting Christian book stores. The
thinking of 150 million members of American churches is being
shaped and transformed by the publications they read, which are
predominantly secular. Christian worldview is formed by the
news and entertainment they watch and read, which is over-
whelmingly secular in choice, interpretation, and presentation.
Consequently, Christian thought today is without biblical vision,
mission, or strategy. It is devoid of any valid spiritual assessment
of existing national or world circumstances, therefore incapable
of biblical worldview development.

The Pastor Who Wasn't Obscure

Many times we find it difficult to be brave for Christ when
it's easier to be obscure. Here is a memorable personal illustra-
tion that speaks to the discipling power of being noticeably
Christian in the culture:

Because our church is quite small, we sometimes have joint
services with two or three other churches in the community. One
such occasion occurred on Good Friday some years ago. The
custom at these shared services is for the pastor from each church
to have a part in the service. On this day, the pastor from the host
church presented the central message. He strayed from the

theme and injected some observations of personal political bias that I felt were an injustice to a national Christian figure I greatly admired. I was inwardly upset and resented the idea that the pulpit was used this way in which no opposing view or defense of my hero could be presented. I remember my continuing, unforgiving discomfort as we left the church and went home. While this man of God did not know me, whenever I read his name or saw him in some public place, my recognition of him was accompanied with the subtle sin of stifled antagonism.

Early in our married life, Phyllis and I initiated the practice of saying grace before all of our meals at home. We honored this observance even when guests of uncertain faith were at our table. However, I am embarrassed to confess that when dining out, we surrendered to cultural conformity and never, repeat, *never*, bowed our heads in prayer over our food in public restaurants. As time passed, the Holy Spirit began to raise the consciousness of my guilt. One evening Phyllis and I were reviewing the dinner menu in one of the local dining places when the unforgiven pastor and his wife sat at a table not more than ten feet away. Of course, he did not know me, but I recognized him immediately and was acutely aware of his presence. A tinge of the old resentment returned.

When finally their food was before them and they were about to begin their meal, he reached across the table and their hands met halfway. They bowed their heads and in the most powerful witness imaginable, he reverently asked God's blessing on their food. My heart was pierced. Even as I write these words, the memory of that scene brings tears to my eyes. From that day to this, Phyllis and I never fail to honor God with our prayerful thanks when we are dining out. They were being identifiably Christian in the culture. By their public witness they were teaching obedience. I was weighed on the scales of God's judgment and found wanting. A few years later, I called him for lunch and shared the experience. We were both moved in the healing presence of the Holy Spirit.

To me, one of the most exciting aspects of Christian potential is faith. We need to have faith that God will use our witness to his glory. It begins with the mysterious, latent power locked inside the kernel of a mustard seed and expands to the magnitude of a mountain-moving, irresistible force. Dormant in the hearts of Christian laity in America is faith sufficient to disciple this nation in one generation! Why should we be intimidated by some theologians whose shortfall of faith cautions us against unrealistic expectations when Jesus calls us to make disciples of all nations? I choose to cast my lot with him to whom all authority has been given on heaven and on earth.

Christian obscurity, paradoxically coupled with a national presence, leaves the body of Christ in America positioned for a spiritual analysis of its *strengths, weaknesses, opportunities,* and *threats:* a diagnosis of biblical understanding essential to laying the groundwork for carrying out Jesus' mandate to disciple our nation, teaching obedience to everything he has commanded. Let us honor the faith of him who empowered us to fulfill the mission of discipling this nation!

If each of us personally does not allow our Christianity to become obscure, if we live it out publicly for all to see and privately for God to see, we will have an impact on the culture.

CHAPTER 4

A SWOT Analysis
of the Body of Christ

PETER DRUCKER IS a name that captures the attention of "cutting edge" business executives. He is one of those authors whose books you buy, not to read but to study. Recognized as the preeminent guru in the management field, Mr. Drucker examines the issues of business management with innate wisdom, intellectual honesty, practical application, always toward defined purpose and targeted results. In his book, *The Effective Executive*, he makes these observations about setting priorities:

"Courage rather than analysis dictates the truly important rules for identifying priorities:

- Pick the future against the past;
- Focus on opportunity rather than on problem;
- Choose your own direction—rather than climb on the bandwagon; and
- Aim high, aim for something that will make a difference, rather than for something that is safe and easy to do."

Mr. Drucker presents a daring thought for Christians to ponder. Achievement depends less on ability than on the courage to go after the opportunity. Rediscovery of these principles by

Christians could initiate a biblical repositioning of the church for the twenty-first century, repositioning where discipling our nation would become the unifying Christ-centered purpose and mission of American Christians, and spiritual transfusion of faith and courage could lead Christians into transition from proclamation emphasis to a mobilization and implementation of discipling resources. The specific purpose would be a discipled nation. Hopefully, those engaged in the endless pursuit of knowing will recognize the equal necessity of doing. There must be a recognized balance between learning and doing. Another of Mr. Drucker's nuggets of truth is the observation that doing things right isn't nearly as important as doing the right things. I find it interesting how closely that gem relates to the biblical assessment of the men of Issachar "who understood the times and knew what Israel should do." Notice how *doing* is the predominant theme in all the above.

No nation in history has ever been so favorably positioned for Great Commission discipling as is the United States at the brink of the twenty-first century. At no time in the 2000 years since Jesus instructed his followers to make disciples of all nations has there been a nation so fervently subjected to proclamation, so effectively confronted, so faithfully prayed over, so prepared for discipling, as is the United States at the close of this century. Sadly, this is also a time when the victorious are ignorant of their proclamation victory and blind to the discipling need and readiness of a people. Our heavenly Father has given American Christians the glorious opportunity to present to him early in the twenty-first century the United States as the first discipled nation.

If you were chosen to represent the body of Jesus Christ in America, can you imagine a higher expression of loving obedience than early in the twenty-first century presenting to God the United States, a discipled nation? A total commitment and mobilization by all Christian denominations to disciple our nation would perfectly honor the love called for in the Great Commandment and be in discipling obedience to the Great Commission of our Lord Jesus Christ. Fulfillment of this biblical mandated vision would epitomize Christian achievement of the vision of God, the mission of Jesus Christ, and the inspired strategies of the Holy Spirit.

VISION is the definition of long-term goal as in "your kingdom come, your will be done on earth as it is in heaven."

MISSION is the central work to be done to accomplish the goal of vision as in "make disciples of all nations by teaching them to obey everything I have commanded you."

STRATEGY is an organized plan of action to do the central work of mission to accomplish the goal of vision as in "But when he, the Spirit of truth comes, he will guide you into all truth. he will not speak on his own; he will speak only what he hears, and he will tell you what is yet to come."

VISION, MISSION, and STRATEGY biblically conceived, designed, and implemented, will reposition the body of Christ in America from where it is today to early in the twenty-first century when, as its chosen emissary, in the ultimate action of loving obedience, you can present to our heavenly Father, the United States, a discipled nation.

Effective planning, productive process development, achieved goals all depend on accurate foundational information. For this reason, we will use a planning process employed successfully in businesses for many years. Known as a SWOT (Strengths, Weaknesses, Opportunities, Threats) analysis, this common business assessment tool will help us understand the current condition of the body of Christ in the United States relevant to Jesus' mandate to disciple our nation. In a SWOT analysis, *Strengths* are defined so their power may be understood and magnified. *Weaknesses* are identified to be overcome and converted to strengths. *Opportunities* are evaluated to determine those that should be vigorously pursued and where valuable resources should be focused. *Threats* need to be understood so they can be neutralized, overcome, or resisted effectively.

STRENGTHS—USE AVAILABLE RESOURCES

Any review of strengths must first identify the spiritual resources available. These are not only formidable but will always be victorious when used in *faith*, *obedience*, and *love*.

The Word of God

Among the greatest strengths of the Christian church in America is its divinely inspired love affair with the Bible. Confirming this, the November 1994 issue of *Emerging Trends*, a publication of the Princeton Religion Research Center, declared the Bible as America's best-read book. The report states, "It is a well-known fact that although it never appears on the best-seller lists, the Bible actually is the perennial best-selling book in this country. Its role in American life seemingly is incalculable. No other book comes even close to having been read by more people, re-read by more people, owned and cherished by more people. By now, so many Bibles have been printed in this country, and continue to be published by the millions each year, that even rough estimates of the total number printed to date do not exist." A June 1993 study by the Gallup Organization established that 81 percent of Americans believe the Bible is either the Word of God or the inspired Word of God.

"The word of God is living and active. Sharper than any double-edged sword, it penetrates even to dividing soul and spirit, joints and marrow; it judges the thoughts and attitudes of the heart" (Hebrews 4:12).

Prayer

The life of Jesus is a flawless human experience modeled for us by the Son of God. One of Jesus' most unnoticed examples was the quality of his prayer life. "After he had dismissed them, he went up into the hills by himself to pray" (Matthew 14:23). He often withdrew to lonely places to pray. Across our nation around the clock, men and women of all ages are at prayer. Volume 3 of *The Barna Report* series finds that nine of ten Americans pray to God. "Eight out of ten adults who engage in prayer say they are 'absolutely certain' that prayer makes a difference in their lives." It has certainly made a difference in mine.

When she was sixty-five, my mother was diagnosed with cancer of the throat. It was surgically removed, and she began a long series of radiation treatments. From the first day we were advised of her condition, I began praying for her healing. Each morning, I privately knelt and asked God to heal her completely. Finally, after two years of praying faithfully every day, one morning I experienced a deep inner assurance of the Holy Spirit that I did not need to continue. She was healed. She died from heart failure ten years later in great peace.

For twenty years, the Wednesday morning prayer meeting at our small church has been loyally attended by Phyllis and a handful of other women. They pray for the pastor and the work of the church. Elected leaders of our nation, regardless of party, are lifted up in prayer. God expects that they serve honorably with wisdom and dignity and look to him for leadership. Members of the congregation and those afflicted and in need are remembered. They praise and thank God for answered prayer. These are prayer warriors on the front lines of a spiritual conflict raging for the soul of our nation. When Phyllis and I are in Florida, we attend a small church in a mainline denomination. Recently a twenty-four hour prayer vigil was held for which pairs signed up for half-hour commitments to pray for the vision and mission of the church leadership and for personal needs of those in the church family who were hurting. A single mother reported afterward that during the prayer watch, her adult son who is schizophrenic and never leaves the house, came to her and said, "Mom, many people are praying for you. They are praying right now. Can you and I pray?" There was inexpressible joy as she added, "This is the first time he has ever mentioned prayer, had an awareness of prayer, showed an interest, or had any desire to participate in prayer."

In a world of selfishness, the sacrificial love of these humble prayer warriors goes largely unrecognized, unreported, and unappreciated. That is, except where it counts most—in the eyes, ears, and heart of a prayer-hearing heavenly Father. These dear ones are also known where their faithfulness is hated and despised, where its power is feared and resented—in the mind of the prince of this world, ruler of the kingdom of darkness. Their names are known and respected by both God and Satan for very different reasons. One of the great strengths of American Christians is that these unsung spiritual combatants exist in thousands of prayer pockets across the nation.

Holy Spirit

My memory is marked by spiritual turning points that led to new meaning in my walk with God. One day, I realized I was hearing conflicting messages about different denominations, angry stories of dissension within churches, antagonism created by hardened doctrinal positions. Self-centered pursuit of vain personal agenda, rather than Holy Spirit leading, seemed to be the driving force in many of these tensions. I was confused and restless in my soul. I did not like what I saw and heard about the Christian walk, and I was far from being at peace with my spiritual direction. I longed for an inner assurance of biblical truth on which I could stand, where I could be at peace with myself, and most of all, be at peace with God. I took my Bible and went before my heavenly Father in prayer. "Dear Lord," I prayed, "I come before you in search of truth. I bring a totally open mind. I am committed not to defend any previously held position. Reveal your truth to me directly. Reveal it through the leading of the Holy Spirit as I read and prayerfully study your Word. I am trusting fully in the power of the Holy Spirit to interpret your Word for me. I understand it will be a spiritual process rather than an event. I am submitting myself to the promise of Jesus where He says, 'But when he, the Spirit of truth, comes, he will guide you into all truth. He will not speak on his own; he will speak only what he hears, and he will tell you what is yet to come'" (John 16:13).

From that day, the Word of God began taking on new meaning for me. I learned that the third person of the Trinity, the Holy Spirit, is one of the most powerful, under-used, under-estimated, least understood, strategic resources available to Christians.

Authority of Jesus Christ

No statement has ever been made that carries such majesty, splendor, and power, as do Jesus' opening words as he presents his final instructions to his disciples and to all future generations of believers. "All authority in heaven and on earth has been given to me" (Matthew 28:18). No person, before or since, has possessed credentials even remotely supporting such a claim. Christians even today do not seem to catch the awesome transfer of authority accomplished in the next two words of the Great Commission. "*Therefore* go." It is not easy for the Christian to get his or her mind around the truth that through the door of *obedience*, Jesus transfers all authority in heaven and on earth to the Christian for the purpose of empowerment, to make disciples by teaching obedience of everything he has commanded us. In teaching obedience, the Christian disciple replicates Jesus Christ in the life of another person. In no other action is God more glorified than in teaching obedience of all Jesus has commanded us, the result of which is the replication of Jesus in the life of another believer.

The power of Christian spiritual resources to favorably impact a degenerate culture may be seen in research conducted some years ago by Harvard University's renowned sociologist, Dr. Pitirim Sorokin. At a time when two of every five marriages in the United States were ending in divorce, Dr. Sorokin determined that in those families who met together daily for Bible study and prayer, the divorce rate was only one in 1,015 marriages! Incredibly, compared to a national divorce rate of 40 percent, in those homes where Christian obedience prevailed in Bible study and prayer, the divorce rate was less than one percent. What an astonishing example of the power of God's Word, the effectiveness of prayer, the truth-revealing presence of the Holy Spirit, and the awesome authority of Jesus Christ!

While we have examined spiritual strengths of American Christianity relative to the Great Commission mandate to disciple our nation, we must not overlook our practical or logistical strengths and the importance of their contribution to the success of our mission.

A National Presence

Late one Saturday afternoon, Phyllis and I were returning home along a suburban route in Lansing we traveled frequently. I turned to her and asked, "Have you ever noticed how many churches there are on this street? I have counted seven in one mile." She nodded and smiled. Obviously the idea pleased her. I was more than pleased; I was intrigued. When we arrived home, I dug out the telephone directory and turned to the Yellow Pages. Finding the church section, I began counting, being care-

ful to avoid duplications of geographic locations or denominational listings. When I completed my work, I couldn't believe
my findings. I counted them again, even more carefully. I was
right the first time—over 450 Christian churches in this mid-
western city—Lansing, Michigan. You had to take in all the
small towns and villages in a twenty-mile radius to come up with
a greater-Lansing area population of 250,000.

My business background began leading me to project what
the resource implications of these numbers might mean on a
national scale. Further research uncovered a national Christian
presence of impressive dimensions—164 denominations, an
amazing 350,000 Christian churches, a membership approaching 150 million, with an annual financial commitment of 56 billion dollars.

Do you think it would be pleasing to God if the stewards of
these resources were united in their understanding of his *Vision*,
" your kingdom come, your will be done on earth as it is in
heaven?" (Matthew 6:10). Do you think it would be pleasing to
Jesus our Lord if the stewards of these resources were united in
their understanding of His *Mission*, "all authority in heaven and
on earth has been given to me. Therefore go and *make disciples*
of all nations, baptizing them in the name of the Father and of
the Son and of the Holy Spirit, and *teaching them to obey everything I have commanded you*. And surely I am with you always, to
the very end of the age" (Matthew 28:18–20 [emphasis mine]).
Imagine the celebration in heaven if American Christians
became united in their biblical discernment of Vision, Mission,
and Strategy and became individually committed to their fulfillment in faith, obedience, and love.

Christian strength in spiritual resources is more than sufficient to fulfill the spiritual requirements of the Great Commission. When added to a national presence and the scope and
depth of material resources available, there is no acceptable

reason why the United States should not become the first discipled nation in human history!

Gifted Pastors

No listing of Christian strengths can be compiled without
listing the teaching giftedness of American pastors and the universal joy they experience in their use of this gift. Three factors
presented by George Barna in his book, *Today's Pastors*, establish
how uniquely and ideally positioned Christian pastors are for
their critical role in fulfilling the mission of a discipled nation in
this generation. In the Barna study, 85 percent of Christian pastors view their knowledge of Scripture as good-to-excellent.
Eighty-three percent list their teaching skills as good-to-excellent. Preaching, teaching and discipling people are three areas of
ministry providing the primary joys in pastoral responsibility.
While the strategic role of these gifts is not yet recognized in the
context of biblical Vision, Mission, and Strategy, their potential
is present, awaiting the inspiration and direction of the Holy
Spirit. Teaching giftedness of pastors is one of the great discipling resources of Christ's church today.

WEAKNESSES—OVERCOME THEM

Surely, a major weakness of the church in America is Christian failure to be engaged in confession and repentance. Individual and personal resistance to the need to humble ourselves
and pray is fed by vanity, pride, and self-centeredness. Those
qualities rise from a generation seeking instant gratification—
physical, material, and spiritual.

Biblical illiteracy leads to spiritual ignorance and self-
righteousness. The deception of self-righteousness leaves the
believer in a condition of unrighteousness filled with residual,
unconfessed, and unforgiven sin. Since God is an administrator

of perfect justice, Christians who walk in the ignorance of unforgiven sin are left without joy, wisdom, spiritual power, and discernment of truth. This is a universal affliction of the body of Christ in America today and probably its major weakness.

Biblical Illiteracy

While the American love affair with the Bible must be considered a major strength in any SWOT analysis of the Christian condition, we must also recognize that Bible numbers do not, by themselves, convert to biblical understanding and obedience. In fact, studies show that less than 17 percent of all Americans read the Bible regularly! It has been observed that 95 percent of the members of evangelical churches would fail to pass a biblical literacy test. We have become a nation of biblical illiterates!

One of the great sorrows of our time and one that must grieve our heavenly Father is the failure of Christians to inspire by example and to communicate a hunger, a thirst, a love, for the infallible truth of God's Word. Carl F. H. Henry in his insightful work, *God, Revelation, and Authority*, says, "The fate of the Bible is the fate of Christianity and even of civilization itself. If the world neglects or evangelicals forsake this book, the end result is society's theological, spiritual and moral suicide."

Christian desire for spiritual nourishment should equal or exceed the need and desire for physical nourishment. The high rate of obesity in the United States results from the affluent Americans' obsession with food. We make sure we fulfill this need *every day*. Food sustains us physically. How then can we explain our casual approach to the biblical nourishment required for the spiritual well-being of our soul, the life of which is eternal. Jesus speaks clearly of this in John 6:58, "This is the bread that came down from heaven. Your forefathers ate manna and died, but he who feeds on this bread will live forever." Again, in history's greatest test of spiritual character, a confrontation took place upon which the future of humankind was at stake. Jesus, in a famished condition after fasting for forty days, is deviously challenged by Satan to turn stones into bread. Jesus answers, "It is written: 'Man does not live on bread alone, but on every word that comes from the mouth of God'" (Matthew 4:4). American Christians may be obese physically, but they are malnourished biblically and consequently, underweight spiritually. A nation of biblical and spiritual lightweights leaves the Christian community in a seriously weakened condition across a broad range of essential Great Commission disciplines.

Absence of Biblical Vision

One of the great needs of the hour is for a unified biblical vision among Christians and their leaders in our nation. Christians require a shared vision so biblically sound, so spiritually demanding, so timely in its application, so responsive to present need, so appropriate to existing circumstances, that it will be universally accepted, supported, and communicated by the Christian community in the United States. Along with the discovery of biblical vision, Christians must recognize biblical mission and understand biblical strategies. Meaning and definition of their respective roles and how they are empowered must be known and communicated.

Vision without a central work is fantasyland. Work without vision becomes drudgery. Vision *with* a central work will change the world. Across all denominations, failure of Christian leadership to recognize the need for a unified biblical vision or a long-term goal, leaves believers wandering aimlessly through a national desert of moral chaos without any specific destination. The Israelites may have had their problems with Moses' leadership, but he always knew their destination was the Promised Land. Absence of effectively communicated biblical vision or a long-term goal denies the Christian community the excitement, the demanding disciplines, the unifying sense of teamwork, the shared victories, the common purpose, the serving experiences, all of which exist in Great Commission obedience and pursuit of the most worthy goal of all: God's divine vision, that *his kingdom come, his will be done on earth as it is in heaven.*

Our heavenly Father does not deal in pie in the sky. He does not call us to unrealistic dreams. He does not challenge us with a vision of a long-term goal that cannot be achieved under the discipline of the three words that form the hallmark of Christian character: *faith, obedience,* and *love.* Nor does he present us divine vision without the essential central work of mission through which his goal is to be achieved. Central work is defined for us by Jesus in the Great Commission. Make disciples by teaching obedience to everything I have commanded you. A pastor friend of mine says he does not use the word *obedience* anymore because in our permissive society, obedience has fallen into disfavor. It signals authority. Perhaps the time has come to replace cultural conformity with leadership courage and trust that in the faith of teaching obedience, Holy Spirit empowerment leading to revelation of truth will take place. After all, this is what Jesus promised. The character attributes related to obedience (such as dignity, honor, faithfulness, self-control, courage, loyalty, discernment) are worthy attitudes, qualities, and disciplines. They mark one as being trustworthy.

Unrighteousness

I'd been having lunch with different community pastors to get their thoughts on the state of the whole church in preparation for doing a SWOT analysis related to the Great Commission. I was dining with the pastor of one of the nearby churches on our side of town. As we finished our lunch, I sensed that this man of God had more to say about the condition of the church in America. I knew that while what he might have to say might

be framed in the context of the church at large, it would be an
agonizing appraisal of his own congregation. Finally, he said,
"Yes, 350,000 churches in the United States is an impressive
number, but the numbers are static. They are not growing.
Dying churches are closing their doors as fast as new churches
are opening theirs." The pain in his heart was evident by the
sadness and bitterness in his voice as he added, "The church in
America is destroying itself from within."

"How so?" I asked, even though I was sure I knew the substance of what his answer would be.

"The problem is that the church is being torn apart by congregational splits. We've had three in our local church in twenty
years, one in the three years that I have been there. A major seg-
ment of the congregation left the church."

We were silent for several moments. I could feel his hurt
and disappointment. The remorse of broken relationships. A
sense of mission failure. The assault on personal faith. Self-
doubt. Then ultimately the searching question, Why? I prayed
for wisdom as I responded, "I've been doing some research on
the weaknesses of the church that causes me to believe that ignorance related to unrighteousness exists throughout the church
today. Unrighteousness caused from the presence of unconfessed
sin in the lives of individuals is the major reason for the dissension and factions so prevalent in the church." He was listening
intently, so I went on, "Few Christians realize that God sees
such behavior as evil as wicked, and that those who foment dissension, factions, and discord are seen in the same light as those
whose hands shed innocent blood. In Proverbs 6:17, among
those things the Lord hates and that are detestable to him are
listed as haughty eyes, a lying tongue, hands that shed innocent
blood and, continuing in Proverbs 6:19, "a man who stirs up dissension among brothers." I described the concepts to be covered
in the next chapter of this book, "Spiritual Transformation—

Gearing Up with Power," and as we parted, he said with obvious conviction, "I know what I'll be teaching in several of my upcoming sermons."

God is going to hold every Christian accountable for his or her personal stewardship in the management of Kingdom resources, which he intended for use in doing the mission work of discipling to achieve his long-term goal of vision. Those who have participated in fomenting dissension, factions, and discord in the church are guilty of wasting the precious Kingdom resources of time, energy, love, harmony, unity, purpose, and direction which are intended by God to be used in the discipling of our nation. The self-centered behavior of these individuals is seen as evil, wicked and satanic in the eyes of a Holy God, and they will be held personally accountable for their sinful, evil behavior. Their blind and wasteful diversion of precious Great Commission resources will not escape the divine administration of God's justice.

Christian Disengagement

While visiting and speaking at churches and conferences in various locations across the country, I am astonished by the number of Christians who do not subscribe to their local newspaper. This phenomenon is only the surface manifestation of more deeply rooted problems of Christian character: withdrawal, timidity, and fear. Some of the reasons given for lack of interest in the local paper invariably relate to negative emphasis of news coverage, anti-Christian bias, lack of a Christian presence, and similar justification. Is this not an abject submission to media intimidation, resulting in a retreat into cultural and psychological isolation? Chalk up another easy victory for the forces of evil— the surrender of another of America's vital institutions to the secular mind. How can we disciple people, applying biblical truths relative to current events, unless we are familiar with current events? How can we *understand the times and know what Christians should do* if we foolishly blindfold ourselves to what is going on around us? "For God did not give us a spirit of timidity, but a spirit of power, of love and of self-discipline" (2 Timothy 1:7).

Believers have disengaged themselves from society as Christians and have reentered as cultural conformists! We have ceased being identifiably Christian (salt and light) in the culture. This is a frightful acknowledgment. It is a devastating confession because it brings us under condemnation because of being ashamed of the One who suffered and died for us, our Savior and Lord, Jesus Christ. We can be assured that Jesus does not take this behavior lightly. He deals with this issue very, very clearly, leaving no doubt about his position regarding those who are embarrassed to be known as one of his followers, "If anyone is ashamed of me and my words, the Son of Man will be ashamed of him when he comes in his glory and in the glory of the Father and of the holy angels" (Luke 9:26).

Lack of Pastoral Vision

The superior strength of pastoral teaching is weakened and dissipated when taken outside the context of biblical vision, mission, and strategy. Instead of Christ-centered unity in teaching designed to support the central work of Christ's mission (Matthew 28:18–20), pastors teach and disciple under independent mission statements, goals, and planning objectives. With 450 churches in the Lansing area, is it not tragic that they are not united under one Christ-centered goal and timetable, a discipled community in our generation? Until pastors are led and directed by biblical vision, mission and strategies, they will continue to be scattered in their teaching.

To list all the additional weaknesses that could be studied here would likely fall under the law of diminishing returns. Our hope, our source of empowerment once again exists in God's Word. As the oppression of our weaknesses bears down upon us, we can lift our eyes in the promise of these words, "In the same way, the Spirit helps us in our weakness. We do not know what we ought to pray for, but the Spirit himself intercedes for us with groans that words cannot express. And he who searches our hearts knows the mind of the Spirit, because the Spirit intercedes for the saints in accordance with God's will. And we know that in all things God works for the good of those who love him, who have been called according to his purpose" (Romans 8:26–28).

Identifying and facing up to our weaknesses is an important step in the analysis process. We must understand our weaknesses and overcome them without becoming diverted from our unwavering focus, which is to become obedient disciples, engaged in making disciples by teaching obedience to everything Jesus has commanded.

OPPORTUNITIES—TAKE ADVANTAGE OF THEM

I drove home with very mixed emotions. It was December 26, 1963, the day after Christmas. I had just submitted my resignation, terminating my employment as sales manager. Of my own volition, I was leaving stable, assured employment and a comfortable, growing income. We had recently moved into our new home with its monstrous mortgage. Four lovely children to feed and clothe added to our need for faith. By our own choice, our monthly income had just plummeted to zero. Because of our growing family, we had accumulated no savings, but our financial picture and credit reputation was A–1 and we intended to keep it that way. We had sold our automobile and replaced it with a leased car, netting $2,500 in cash. Another $2,500 borrowed from the bank enabled us to put up $5000 capital for our new business. We cleared out an extra bedroom, installed a $35 used wooden desk and a telephone, and one week later on January 2, 1964, Russell Business Forms, Inc. was launched as a

Michigan corporation. It was incorporated from the first day because we had always perceived this new enterprise as a vision of substance, intrinsic value, and growth. Others might ask why anyone would submit himself or herself and a family to the uncertainty of such risks. The answer is a timeless one—because of faith, challenge, and hope. Yes, tremendous risks existed, but always more powerful than the fear was the inner faith, the vision, the irresistible unseen force that beckoned—*opportunity*!

Think Positively

The first days, weeks, and months, even years of building a new business from ground zero are filled with countless problems never before experienced by the entrepreneur. They are times of extremely limited resources, especially time and money. Knowing that 50 percent of all new business start-ups fail in their first year and 85 percent will have collapsed by the end of the second year imposes a survival stress on the small-business owner that defies accurate description. Having personally lived through this traumatic test of faith, I know that attitude control is absolutely critical to survival. Called "self-control" in the Bible, it is one of the fruits of the Holy Spirit. Whenever another setback occurred, I reminded myself that, Within every defeat is the seed of an equivalent or greater victory. To believe this with profound conviction is to maintain an attitude of optimism. The biblical truth undergirding this power principle is established in Romans 8:26, "And we know that in all things God works for the good of those who love him, who have been called according to his purpose."

Get a Vision

The 15 percent of small business owners that survive beyond the two-year wipe-out, are invariably those who maintain a positive perspective and who hold a clearly focused vision or long-term goal for their company. They support their focused vision with a superior understanding of their mission or the central work to be performed and pursued an enlightened strategy or organized plan to take their product or service to market. American Christianity has an intergalactic-sized, black-hole vacuum of such leadership, and therein lies a magnificent discipling opportunity!

The goal-achievement system of *Vision-Mission-Strategy* is not a business-success principle or a military-victory principle. It is a biblical achievement principle! It is a universally effective, biblical, goal-achievement system. It can be as effectively applied in discipling our nation as in reaching the long-term goals of a small business. The difference is one of scale. I speak from thirty-one years' experience in corporate profitability and ten years' experience in successfully establishing the discipling presence of God's Word in the secular print media through the Amy Foundation, Amy Writing Awards program, and its offshoot, the Church Writing Group Movement. Today, because of the application of this biblical goal-achievement system, through the Amy Foundation, thousands of people across our nation will read biblical truth reinforced with Scripture in the secular-print media. This will happen not only today but every day this year and each day for the foreseeable future. The effective results of spiritual laws founded upon biblical truth are as immutable, as predictable, as physical laws.

In preparation for the twenty-first century, the historical opportunity for Christians exists in recognizing that discipling our nation is an achievable goal. Who will effectively oppose the followers of Jesus Christ when in a unity of faith, obedience, and love they mobilize their spiritual and material resources to disciple this nation? Their ultimate God-glorifying victory becomes undeniable when undertaken in the context of biblical VISION, MISSION, AND STRATEGY and when effective communication of these truths becomes the faith-centered priority of Christian leaders and writers.

One of the characteristics setting Christianity apart from all other religions is that it alone has a worldwide presence. Of all the world's Christians, those in America have been given the unparalleled opportunity to present to our heavenly Father a discipled nation in this generation! Faithful proclamation of the gospel for hundreds of years has resulted in the national uniqueness of a people where 85 percent believe in the life, death, resurrection, and spiritual existence of Jesus Christ. In the United States, the proclamation victory has been won! The discipling failure has yet to be discovered, defined, and overcome! What Jesus requires from his followers now is the obedience to produce the victory of a discipled nation!

Every believer must be challenged by the need to become an obedient disciple and to make disciples by teaching believers to obey everything Jesus has commanded. A national redirection and mobilization of Christian resources focusing on obedience to the Great Commission, defined by Jesus in Matthew 28:18–20, will enable American Christians early in the twenty-first century to proclaim to the world, "Blessed is our nation whose God is the Lord."

Confronting every American believer is the glorious opportunity to be a Christ-centered servant, an obedient disciple, a model of wisdom in the grandest of all causes—the demanding, sacrificial work of discipling our nation by making disciples and teaching obedience to everything Jesus has commanded. If the country is discipled as it should be, all other biblically supported goals—political, economic, spiritual, moral, or cultural—would be accomplished.

THREATS: WATCH OUT FOR SATAN

A national epidemic of biblical illiteracy centered in the Christian community is among the gravest threats to the victory called for in Christ's Great Commission mandate. It leads to believer ignorance of spiritual warfare and causes a subliminal denial of personal involvement in the spiritual conflict always within and around us. The loss of this momentous struggle portends terrible consequences, both personal and national, and must be recognized as a major threat to the cause of a discipled nation.

Failure of Christians to credit Satan with having the basic intelligence, the evil genius, the vision, or diabolical cleverness to have in place a national strategy designed to divert and neutralize Christian vitality, if continued, will consign our nation to the historical junkpile of all previous immoral and degenerate nations. The truth is that Satan's plan is working so well, and Christians are proving to be so docile and submissive, that he is unlikely to change his overall strategy any time soon.

Satan's grand strategy is continued diversion of Christ's Great Commission discipling resources into the nearly fruitless ongoing pursuit of a biblical goal long ago achieved in the United States—the goal of proclamation victory to which Christians aspire. Satan smiles as he watches us continue to pour untold energy and valuable time along with spiritual and material resources into the effort of producing "decisions" when clearly 85 percent of Americans have already "decided." They said yes.

Jesus' life and witness placed far greater emphasis on being an obedient disciple and making disciples by teaching obedience rather than on producing the result described in the word *decisions* as used by many Christians today. The *NIV Exhaustive Concordance* does not show a single listing of the word *decisions* in the context being used by millions of Christians today, while there are 295 listings of the word *disciple*, singular and plural, and 258 listings of the word *obey* and its variants. As a Christian who loves truth and who feels compelled to present to the Holy Spirit an open mind to truth, I find the combined number of 553 biblical

listings of the words *disciple* and *obedience*, compared to zero listings of the word *decisions*, as used in modern Christian context,
to be a powerful statement about their relative significance. To
me, the conclusion that Christian attention and resources continue to be diverted by our common enemy, Satan is reinforced.

Jesus' Temptation and Victory

To better understand the times and the nature of spiritual
warfare being waged for the soul of our nation, we should begin
by reviewing Satan's temptation of our Lord in the desert. Three
individual assaults took place. Each was carefully planned and
designed to appeal to the vulnerabilities of the human condition.
Interestingly, Satan's first attack was directed to the needs and
desires of the flesh. Jesus was famished. He had gone forty days
without eating. Weakened and exhausted, Satan entreats him to
turn the stones into bread. Jesus answers, "It is written: 'Man
does not live on bread alone, but on every word that comes from
the mouth of God'" (Matthew 4:4). Biblical illiteracy does not
cut it when we are engaged in spiritual conflict with the Prince
of Darkness. In the spiritual conflict raging for the direction of
our lives and for the soul of our nation, believers must recognize
the flesh and its vulnerabilities as a primary battleground. Confronted by Jesus with biblical truth and rejected by the spirit of
self-control, Satan moves to the next level.

Vanity, pride, self-centeredness—all are related to the
human ego. Satan's understanding of the human craving for ego
gratification is second to none. He takes our Lord to the highest point of the temple. With heavy emphasis on the very first
word, he says, "If you are the Son of God, throw yourself down.
For it is written: 'He will command his angels concerning you,
and they will lift you up in their hands, so that you will not strike
your foot against a stone.'" Jesus answers him, "It is also written:
'Do not put the Lord your God to the test.'" By implying that

Jesus may not be the Son of God, but being able to prove his divinity to Satan by leaping from the top of the temple, Satan is not only appealing to human vanity but is also distorting Scripture to deceive and tempt our Lord into a demonstration of sinful pride and vanity. Once again Jesus effectively defends himself with the belt of scriptural truth.

Having failed twice, the Prince of Darkness finally makes his major move. Humans crave glory, power, and control over others. Desire for control begins early in life. Even when only two are involved, the urge for dominance asserts itself subtly, overtly, and blatantly. Always deceptively. Passion for power to control others is the opposite of a servant's heart. Satan knows that Jesus had been given all authority in heaven and on earth, and he also knows that Jesus did not come to be served but to serve and to give his life as a ransom for many. He moves to corrupt the serving heart of the Son of God.

"Again, the devil took him to a very high mountain and showed him all the kingdoms of the world and their splendor. 'All this I will give you,' he said, 'if you will bow down and worship me.'"

Jesus says to him, "Away from me, Satan! For it is written: 'Worship the Lord your God, and serve him only.' Then the devil left him, and angels came and attended him" (Matthew 4:8–11). Here Jesus not only defends himself but in using the sword of the spirit, which is the Word of God, he went on the offensive and ordered Satan's departure. The lesson of Jesus' successful defense and the ultimate victory that drove Satan away was his total knowledge *and use* of Scripture in obedience to his heavenly Father.

Beware of Temptations

Desires of the flesh, vanity, glory in the power of control over others—the Devil uses these temptations effectively against you and me. These three building blocks of sin form a triad of human vulnerability through which Christians are losing battle after battle as Satan presses his strategy to win the spiritual war being waged for the soul of America.

Every church in the United States is a critical battleground where Satan and his spiritual minions are at work, deceptively inspiring the destructive behavior in Christians that leads to the important local victories for the forces of evil. Dominance by Satan of individuals or groups within the church results in the following behaviors. These become important resources for the forces of evil. Here are a few: dissension, factions, discord, selfish ambition, vain personal agenda, distractions, anger, unforgiven resentments, gossip, and many others. When Christians are guilty of these wicked behaviors, Satan is successfully diverting discipling resources of time and energy into his worldly kingdom. The family of God is being effectively immobilized, diverted, and lured into busyness instead of fruitfulness.

Strengths, weaknesses, opportunities, threats—an analysis of the condition of the Christian church in America today. More than anything, this higher understanding leads me to an attitude of hope. I am more deeply convinced that the spiritual attributes presented by Jesus' example—faith, obedience, and love—will provide the energy and power required to disciple our nation. Studying these qualities daily in Scripture, applied in the framework of biblical vision, mission, and strategy, will once again turn the world upside down. It has its beginning in the heart of every American Christian when he or she says, "Starting now, I must personally participate in the greatest of all causes, The United States, a discipled nation in this generation."

Jesus calls every Christian to righteousness rising from obedience. How this will happen is discussed in the next chapter, "Spiritual Transformation . . . Gearing up with Power."

CHAPTER 5

Spiritual Transformation:
Gearing Up with Power

THE LETTER WAS handwritten and unexpected. It came from a young man who worked in our warehouse until he graduated from high school. He was tall, maybe 6'2", and soft-spoken. In his late teens, he had problems trying to find himself and maintain civility with his parents. There were rumors of unpredictable and wild behavior. I had talked to him occasionally about my faith in Jesus Christ. Phyllis and I gave him a Bible for graduation. He was probably twenty-one and gone from our employment about three years when the letter arrived. These are the exact words.

Dear Mr. Russell:

God has really changed my life. He's taken away all of the dirt and garbage from my life and replaced it with love and happiness. There is an area God has shown me that I must deal with. There were times when I worked for you I took supplies home and never returned them. This was before I gave my life to Jesus. But God told me I had to correct this wrong. It was difficult to write this letter and ask your forgiveness after so long a time. Enclosed is the amount the Lord

directed me to send to you. I pray that God continues
to bless you and your company. I encourage you to keep
sharing Jesus boldly. It took a while to soften my heart,
but I've never regretted giving my life to Jesus. Every
day is real exciting being with the Lord. He gives me
great peace and joy. Again please forgive me and God
bless you and your family.

> Your brother in Jesus, Michael

A Travelers Express Money Order was enclosed for $27.80.
Michael and his wife have been foreign missionaries for several years. They are presently in Nepal, providing desperately
needed training for local pastors. Nepal is a country not
renowned for its friendly support for Christian missionaries.

UNCONFESSED SIN

Earlier we asked how is it possible for our nation to experience such an accelerating moral decline when 89 percent of
Americans perceive themselves as Christians and 85 percent
believe in the life, death, and resurrection and spiritual existence
of Jesus Christ. Obviously, a huge behavioral difference exists
between being merely a believing Christian and being an obedient Christian walking intimately with the Lord. Since believers
enjoy an established presence in all aspects of our culture, the
tragedy of our spiritual and moral decline results from a breakdown of biblical obedience in the lives of individual Christians.
If believers do not permit God to control their inner lives, how
can they expect to be effective and courageous to influence the
morality of cultural life around us?

In the transition to accountability and self-examination, the
question I asked earlier bears repeating. Is there a universal
unconfessed sin draining spiritual power and effectiveness from

the body of Christ in America today? I was driven to ask that question of myself several years ago because of four great loves in my life: Love for God, love for Jesus Christ, love for my wife and family, and love for this divinely blessed nation and its magnificent Christian heritage. One day, mindful of that question and yearning to determine a biblical answer, I read a passage of Scripture many consider to be God's divine prescription for the healing of a nation: "if my people, who are called by my name, will humble themselves and pray, and seek my face and turn from their wicked ways, then will I hear from heaven and will forgive their sin and will heal their land" (2 Chronicles 7:14). As I read that soul-confronting passage again and pondered the profound significance of its healing promise, I knew there was more here than most Christians realize. For several days I prayed over and memorized those words. Their timeliness and relevance were impressed upon me as the truth-revealing work of the Holy Spirit was being accomplished in my heart, mind, and soul. I knew there was fresh insight for today's Christian in the ageless truth of these captivating words from God. Finally it came.

How many Christians have you heard recently confess to being wicked? How many even believe they are wicked? Most Christians do not perceive themselves as wicked. Is this a problem? When asked if they are sinners, their answers change dramatically. Christians know they are sinners and readily confess it. Such willing acknowledgment raises new questions. If I am not a wicked sinner, does that mean I'm basically a nice sinner? Does it mean I'm a cultured sinner, an educated sinner, a refined sinner, a good sinner, an average sinner, a B+ sinner? Has God changed his standard of sin? Is the condition of sin no longer wicked in the eyes of a holy God? Deep down in the inner recesses of our heart, we know better. All sin is wicked in his eyes.

Here is a profound truth. Christians have reinterpreted the biblical definition of wickedness and sin. They have defined a category of sins for themselves they consider only naughty or at least acceptable to accommodate their shameful surrender to the conformity of a worldly culture.

We can readily see that Christians do not perceive themselves as wicked because, for the most part, they are not participating in what the Christian community chooses to define as the wicked sins of our day, such as assault, theft, murder, violence, adultery, addiction, abusive and profane language, and a host of other actions seen as wicked and ugly.

We are led to a tragic conclusion—Christians do not see themselves as wicked; they do not see their righteousness as filthy rags; they do not see themselves as needing to be in a state of ongoing confession and repentance. The result is that the body of Christ in America today is, in large part, suffering from the power-draining effect of a universally unconfessed sin . . . The vanity of self-righteousness!

THE DANGERS OF SUBTLE SIN

The vanity of self-righteousness is subtle, satanic, devious, and immobilizing. It causes us to focus on the minor issues and trivialities. It causes us to hide behind a shield of skepticism, indifference, and cynicism. It causes us to contrive weak and flimsy excuses for not attending church and for not being engaged in discipling the believers. It causes us to engage in the evil and wicked pursuit of dissensions and factions within the local church, resulting in wasteful diversion of Great Commission resources. This resource diversion is exactly as planned by the father of all liars.

- This subtle sin prevents us from seeing ourselves as we really are.
- This subtle sin prevents us from humbling ourselves, seeking his holy face and turning from our wicked ways.

- This subtle sin prevents us from the repentant, heartfelt prelude to power that comes when we cry out in anguish, "God have mercy on me, a sinner" (Luke 18:13).
- This subtle sin prevents us from seeing our need to be in an ongoing state of confession and repentance.
- This subtle sin prevents us from experiencing the righteousness that comes from having no unconfessed sin in our lives.

This subtle sin prevents us from living in obedience to the Word of God and experiencing the Holy Spirit's power that flows from righteousness. Residual unconfessed sin leaves us in disobedience, without spiritual power, and unable to influence a world crying out for discipling, a world desperately in need of being taught obedience to everything he has commanded us.

God in his loving graciousness provides us with a most wonderful solution to our predicament and subsequent lack of power. For it is through Jesus Christ that, "If we confess our sins, he is faithful and just and will forgive us our sins and purify us from all unrighteousness" (1 John 1:9). Notice an astonishing fact. If we confess the sins of which we are aware, he forgives those specifically, and purifies us from *all* unrighteousness. All other residual sins are also forgiven. When we are cleansed from all unrighteousness, we become righteous. When we are in a state of righteousness with no unconfessed sin in our lives, *blatant or subtle*, the Holy Spirit works through us, impacting the lives of others with discipling power—a discipling power following the vision and loving compassion of our prayer life.

For us to fulfill Great Commission vision, we need to identify, confess, and repent from the subtle sins in our lives that go unrecognized and unconfessed.

Take a subtle sin inventory of your life—when did you last experience deep remorse, confession, and repentance of these sins? If you haven't, these sins are a barrier preventing the Holy Spirit from working through you in discipling power. Be reminded, to repent means to turn away in sorrow!

During the time I was prayerfully coming to understand this new meaning of 2 Chronicles 7:14, my concern mounted for the unconfessed subtle sins in my own walk. I became more sensitive to my own personal problem of subtle sin. Among others, I realized vanity as a constant thorn pricking my conscience. I could see how important it was to identify the sins I committed daily, even hourly; sins I committed with little or no awareness, concern, or remorse on my part. I thought to myself, *I know I am guilty of at least six or seven that should be confessed instantly when they occur, so I can replace them with faith, obedience and love.* My list began with vanity, pride, impatience, lukewarmness, indifference, anxiety, and skepticism. I winced as they came to mind almost too quickly, and I pressed on. There must be more. I kept writing. Soon I had filled a complete column on a standard letter-sized sheet of paper. I knew I was on to something. Over the days and weeks following, I discovered many more attitudes and actions that I found to be biblically sinful. Yes, they might be considered to be of the subtle variety, but they were very, very real. Subtle sins are stealthy and debilitating. They move like an undiagnosed cancer through Christian character, destroying the potential for discipling in loving obedience.

God is not particularly interested in how those he has created define sin. He has already done that. All sin is offensive to a holy God. All sin is evil. All sin is wicked. All sin is disobedience. All sin violates his perfect holiness. Three dimensions of the character of God are of eternal importance to every person who has ever lived, because all except Jesus Christ have sinned. First, he is a God of absolute holiness and righteousness. Second, he is a God of lovingkindness. He expresses his character of holy righteousness in the action of loving-kindness. Many

Christians end their analysis of God at that point. They make a terrible, tragic mistake. A third dimension of God is that he is an administrator of *perfect justice*. Every sin that has ever been committed by you and me or anyone else, past, present and future, must be accounted for. It must be either punished or it must be forgiven. There are no alternatives. Period. God's sense of perfect justice will not permit any act of sin to escape accountability. He is a God of absolute holiness! He is a God of lovingkindness! He is a God of perfect justice! "For God so loved the world that he gave his one and only Son, that whoever believes in him shall not perish but have eternal life" (John 3:16).

After several months, my list of subtle sins grew to three columns and totaled fifty-seven. There are many more, but this is enough to make our point. Here is a list.

Subtle Sins

Addiction	Egotism
Anger	Envy
Animosity	Factions
Bitterness	Fear
Boastfulness	Gluttony
Closed-Mindedness	Gossip Indulgence
Condemnation	Guilt
Judgment	Hatred
Condescension	Haughtiness
Covetousness	Hostility
Critical Nature	Idolatry
Depression	Immoral Fantasies
Discord	Impatience
Discouragement	Impurity
Dissension	Indifference
Dogmatism	Inflexibility
Domination	Insincerity

Intemperance	Rebellion
Jealousy	Resentment
Lack of Affection	Rudeness
Laziness	Self-Righteousness
Lukewarmness	Selfish Ambition
Materialism	Selfishness
Negativism	Unbelief, Lack of Faith
Prayerlessness	Unforgiveness
Prejudice	Ungratefulness
Pride	Vanity
Purposelessness	

A plague of subtle, unconfessed sin, blanketed by a universal condition of self-righteousness, blinds United States Christians to biblical vision, mission, and strategy and sucks the spiritual energy from their need to disciple others. Satan is delighted at the ease with which Christians are media-intimidated and gleeful at their unbiblical retreat into cultural isolation. Passive submission should be unthinkable when access to *all authority in heaven and on earth* is as near as heart, mind, soul, tongue, and Bible, as near as confession and repentance.

Long before the Holy Spirit revealed the issue of subtle sin in my life, Satan was using it effectively to divert my creative energy and discipling resources into the arena of personal antagonisms where he reigns supreme.

THE NEW PASTOR: AN ILLUSTRATION OF
SUBTLE SIN

A new pastor had arrived at our church, and I was finding the transition much more difficult than I had anticipated. Phyllis and I were in our late twenties, and we'd been drawn to this church because of the obvious love for Christ the young pastor had exhibited. We first attended his church when he led the marriage ceremony of a friend of ours. While we didn't know if she was a believer, spiritual sensitivity dominated the memory of the wedding. For seven years, our faith grew under the spiritual mentoring of this young man of God. His style reflected his youth, and everyone called him by his first name. This was our first church as young adults, and we were comfortable, enjoying becoming part of the family of God. Gradually and almost unnoticed by us, Christian character development was taking place in our lives. Then suddenly it changed. Our friend, our counselor, our pastor accepted a call to another church on the West Coast.

The new pastor was very different. He was much older. His style was quite formal. His communication was carefully precise. He invoked a liturgical worship. He selected hymns that were ponderous, stiff, ancient, solemn, and dirge-like. And of all things, he insisted on being addressed as "reverend"! I could handle everything but the "reverend" part. I noticed that he called me Jim. I began to resent that. If he required us to address him as "reverend," he should call me "Mr. Russell." After the initial subtle sin of resentment became established in my heart and mind, the rest came easily. A pastor may be more vulnerable in the area of sermon quality than in most any other facet of his job description. Before long, his Sunday messages became practically meaningless to me. I picked them apart in great detail. Very little escaped. His logic was flawed. The delivery was drab. Scripture references didn't apply. Conclusions were weak or nonexistent. He really didn't have a chance. This went on for some months, and I became increasingly miserable. One redeeming aspect to this sorry and shameful episode is that I did not share these selfish, evil, sinful thoughts and attitudes with any other person. Not even with Phyllis.

Confession Frees Us from Satan's Influence

Since I submit to the discipline of reading the Bible every day, the Holy Spirit has the opportunity to reveal eternal truth to me daily. Under his prompting, I slowly came under the conviction that my attitude toward the new pastor was wrong. He was a man of God, dearly beloved by our heavenly Father. This man had given his entire life to serving the Lord. He was faithful and devoted. I was ashamed. I knew I had wronged him. I began praying for him. I asked God to bless his ministry at our church. I asked God to bless his family and all those dear to him. I asked God to empower his Sunday messages with the Holy Spirit. I confessed my sin and asked God to forgive me. As I continued praying for him, the weeks passed, and something wonderful happened. Jesus replaced the animosity in my heart with a spirit of love for the pastor. Soon I began to receive spiritual insight and discernment from his sermons that I knew came from the Holy Spirit, because like most men of God, his messages were always biblically inspired, prayerfully supported, and presented in faith. He presented truth if listeners were willing to hear with spiritual ears.

As I scan the list of subtle sins, identifying those I committed during the months of tension, I marvel at the clever genius of our Enemy. How deceptively he spins the web of subtle, unconfessed sin through our lives until we are living in obedience to the Enemy of the Father instead of obedience to the Son of the Father, our Lord Jesus Christ. Many were the subtle sins I was guilty of in my animosity toward our new pastor. These sins were a betrayal of my faith in God and placed me in the camp of the Enemy. They were animosity, bitterness, closed mindedness, condemnation, judgment, condescension, critical nature, egotism, haughtiness, hostility, impatience, inflexibility, insincerity, jealousy, lack of affection, lukewarmness, negativism, prayerlessness, prejudice, pride, rebellion, resentment, self-righteousness, selfishness, skepticism, unbelief, unforgive-ness, ungratefulness, and vanity. I am sure there are many oth-ers. Can there be any doubt that while I was controlled by these attitudes and thoughts, I was honoring Satan, serving the forces of evil, and no way could I be effectively obedient to the disci-pling mission of Jesus Christ? *If I had shared these thoughts and attitudes with only one other person in the church, what further sub-tle sins would have been added to this litany of shame?* Here are some: Anger, boastfulness, discord, discouragement, dissension, dogmatism, factions, gossip, and guilt. If I had begun to tell others of my feelings of resentment, vanity and pride would have made it far more difficult to confess and repent the error of my ways. Satan cleverly uses entrapment to enlarge the cir-cle of discontent.

We can be assured that today thousands of variations of this subtle sin scenario are being lived out in each of the 350,000 Christian churches across the nation. In fact, so serious is this debacle of personal antagonism, dissension, and factions, they seriously impede the Great Commission mandate. How can this be when we are to be known as Christians by our deep, abiding, sacrificial love for one another?

Let the Holy Spirit Take Control

We have just reviewed the consequences when the spirit of Satan rules our lives. Behavioral consequences and lifestyle are so victoriously different when the Holy Spirit controls our lives. We marvel that believers would casually choose to be biblically illiterate and ignorant of their life-changing importance! "But when the Holy Spirit controls our lives he will produce this kind of fruit in us: love, joy, peace, patience, kindness, goodness, faithfulness, gentleness and self-control. Those who belong to Christ have nailed their natural evil desires to his cross and cru-cified them there. If we are living now by the Holy Spirit's power, let us follow the Holy Spirit's leading in every part of our lives" (Galatians 5:22–25 TLB).

Imagine, if instead of being hospitable to Satan's spirit of subtle sin, I had instantly made the free-will choice, (which I did later) of submitting to Holy Spirit control and enabled him to produce fruit in my life related to the arrival of the new pastor. What a completely different, Christ-honoring experience it would have been. Instead of anger, I would have had love. Animosity would have been replaced by kindness. Anxiety by peace. Bitterness by love, joy, and kindness. Closed-mindedness by patience and gentleness. Condemnation by love and kindness. Judgment by goodness and love. Condescension by gentleness and love. Critical nature by kindness. Depression by joy. Discord by peace. The entire transition process from old to new pastor would have been one dominated by the fruit of the Holy Spirit—love, joy, peace, patience, kindness, goodness, faithfulness, gentleness, and self control.

Following spiritual transformation through confession and repentance, *gearing up with power* becomes the order of the day. Spiritual power arriving through the character of *righteousness* must be directed to the work of Mission as defined by our Lord. The entire body of Christ in America must pray every day for *the United States, a discipled nation in this generation.* We need to use every available means to deepen our faith and become more effective in working for the Lord. In 2 Peter 1:5–8, the transformed apostle gives us these marvelous instructions: "For this very reason, make every effort to add to your faith goodness; and to goodness, knowledge; and to knowledge, self-control; and to self-control, perseverance; and to perseverance, godliness; and to godliness, brotherly kindness; and to brotherly kindness, love. For if you have these qualities in increasing measure, they will keep you from being ineffective and unproductive in your knowledge of our Lord Jesus Christ."

Peter says, "make every effort." To me, that means we are to work very hard at it. What is the end result of possessing these qualities in an increasing measure? We will become *effective and productive in our knowledge of Jesus Christ.* No other meaning can be attached to this passage than to make disciples of others as Jesus has commanded. To me, that is the epitome of fulfillment of the love called for in the Great Commandment and the obedience called for in the Great Commission.

Take a subtle sin inventory of your life! Write your sins down. Do it prayerfully. Take several days. Add to your list whenever you discover another in your daily reading of Scripture. Add blatant sins as well. Spiritual transformation for the reader will take place with confession and repentance. Previously unconfessed sin will be replaced with righteousness. Righteousness is followed with Holy Spirit power. Spiritual harmony of righteousness and power is confirmed in James 5:16, "Therefore confess your sins to each other and pray for each other so that you may be healed. The prayer of a righteous man is powerful and effective." Spiritual transformation, gearing up with power in your life is as close as confession and repentance.

Within the biblical context of human history related to God's Vision, his mission as defined by Jesus Christ, and strategies inspired by the Holy Spirit, the importance of the whole process of spiritual transformation—gearing up with power exists in its empowerment of m*ission*. Elimination of unconfessed sin in the local church opens the gates of heaven to the inexhaustible resources embodied in the credential-establishing declaration with which the King of kings announced the Great Commission, "All authority in heaven and on earth has been given to me, therefore go,"

When spiritual transformation of the local church imbues it with a biblical worldview and an individual central purpose, spiritually energized in its focus on making disciples by teaching obedience of all he has commanded us, the American church will be engaged in fulfilling its biblical and eternal destiny. And with great power.

Understanding of subtle sin and its consequences, coupled with revelation of the vanity of self-righteousness as a universal unconfessed sin prepares the way to spiritual transformation—gearing up with power.

The arrival of the end of the twentieth century also brings an appropriate time to discard trivial irrelevance and fruitless processes. Methods, old and tired, need to be replaced with the new, the fresh, the effective and productive. This is a time for new concepts in time for a new century and a new era. Realignment of Paradigms—a Christian Imperative.

CHAPTER 6

Realignment of Paradigms . . . A Christian Perspective

NOTHING IS AS inevitable as change. Not one iota of progress can be made without change. No worthy goal, personal or national, to which Christians aspire, is achievable without significant change. Declining influence of the church in American life can in large measure be attributed to the Christian's desire to cling to tired, outmoded, comfortable, ineffective, and obsolete paradigms. Christian fear and resistance to change has rendered it nearly irrelevant in shaping the direction of the nation's vital institutions. America changes, and Christians stagnate.

What is a paradigm? Trend forecaster, Joel Barker, describes the paradigm as a "Grid of values and rules through which we interpret and understand our life." In his book, *Discovering the Future: The Business of Paradigms*, Mr. Barker leads us to recognize how we get locked into obsolete and unproductive thinking. Human tendency is to cling to the comfortable, the traditional, the easy procedures and programs regardless of diminishing or nonexistent returns. But understanding of old and new paradigms fosters fresh and enlightened thinking.

A newsletter for leaders of growing churches by Win Arn headlined this question: *Paradigms—Are They Working for Or Against You?* It says that paradigms provide structures for solving our problems and strategies for accomplishing our goals.

Paradigms are why we do things and how we think they should be done. They are the lenses through which we see and interpret our world.

Mr. Arn continues that the church is also struggling between old and new paradigms. The struggle is crucial because the outcome will determine whether the church has an influence in American's lives into the twenty-first century or becomes a relic of the past. He points to the empty churches in Europe and the unchurched population that shows the consequences of the church's holding on to old paradigms as the world around it changes. Yet many church leaders are not even aware that the church—even their church—is facing such a crucial point in its history.

The report continues that as times change, paradigms often change. The tip-off is when the paradigm no longer works to accomplish the original mission. Either a new paradigm must be found that provides a new and effective process of goal achievement, or the old paradigm is retained that leads to increasing irrelevance and eventually, obsolescence.

The Christian challenge in this book lies in its call to obedience to the final instructions of our Lord as presented in the Great Commission, "make disciples of all nations, teaching them to obey everything I have commanded you" (Matthew 28:18–20). In the human limitations of my mind, I can conceive of no higher glorification of God than living in obedience to the mandate of our Lord, which calls us to be an obedient disciple and to make disciples by teaching obedience to everything he has commanded us. This is the ultimate expression of love called for in the Great Commandment. In the spirit of Great Commission obedience, we will examine old paradigms that are ill-conceived, outdated, irrelevant, and ineffective and present paradigms to replace them—new paradigms biblically applicable to Christians and the church as we approach the dawn of the twenty-first century.

CHANGE YOUR PARADIGMS

Defining and embracing new paradigms is an exciting process. Many years ago before the word *paradigm* became recognized as a goal-achievement process, Phyllis and I wrote our lifetime goals. In one sentence, we designed a Christ-centered, Christ-controlled destiny of effective productivity. We committed ourselves to daily prayer for the realization of the goals we envisioned. From that day forward, we entered a new lifetime paradigm. It influenced the character of our decision making. Every decision was shaped and formed in the light of how it would impact our mission statement. It caused us to remain focused on our Christ-centered lifetime goals. "If you believe, you will receive whatever you ask for in prayer" (Matthew 21:22).

Personal

Old: I'm basically a good Christian.

New: I am a self-righteous sinner. My life is filled with unconfessed, blatant, and subtle sin.

Old: The Christian today is a passive believer, with little or no influence in the culture.

New: The Christian today must become an obedient believer in Christ-centered love, making a discipling difference in family, church, community, and the culture at large.

Old: I pray each day. Almost every one does.

New: I not only pray daily but in loving spontaneity throughout the day on issues large and small, in praise and thanksgiving, in concern and intercession, and most important, in confession and repentance.

Old: I read the Bible often.

New: I read the Bible daily. As the human body requires physical nourishment daily, the eternal well-being of my soul requires the spiritual nourishment of biblical truth daily.

Old: I think I'm as happy as most people.

New: Through daily confession and repentance of the blatant and subtle sins in my life, I am at peace with God and enjoy the blessings of the nine fruits of the Holy Spirit: love, joy, peace, patience, kindness, goodness, faithfulness, gentleness, and self-control.

Old: My central purpose in life is to be a good Christian.

New: My central purpose in life is to glorify God by being an obedient disciple and to make disciples, beginning with my spouse and family.

Old: I am basically good. My decent lifestyle is my Christian witness.

New: I must be publicly and identifiably Christian in the culture. My lifestyle must honor Jesus Christ. It must be visibly and overtly a discipling witness, a teaching witness. As a Christian, I am called to make a discipling difference in the culture.

Old: I am comfortable in my relationship with God.

New: I must love God with all my heart, mind, and soul and continue growing in this love emotionally, intellectually, and spiritually. I am commanded to express my love for God in a life of discipling service to others.

Old: What can one person do?

New: "Now glory be to God, for by his mighty power at work within us is able to do far more than we would ever dare to ask or even dream of. Infinitely beyond our highest prayers, desires, thoughts, or hopes" (Ephesians 3:20 TLB).

Old: Discipling is for the religious professionals.

New: Here am I, Lord, send me!

Old: I don't know anything about discipling.

New: One of life's great joys is discipling another person in a one-on-one situation. (Excellent discipling guides are available for this purpose such as the Operation Timothy manual produced by The Navigators.)

Old: There are no organized discipling groups in the local church.

New: I disciple thousands in our community in the local print media through our Church Writing Group.

The Local Church

Old: Our vision is defined and combined with our mission statement. It's very good.

New: Vision is a long-term goal that is distinctly different from mission. Jesus clearly defined God's vision for his church. God's long-term goal for his church was presented by Jesus in these words, "Your kingdom come, your will be done on earth as it is in heaven" (Matthew 6:10). God's kingdom comes when his will is done by an obedient and righteous people.

Old: Every church should have a mission statement. Ours was developed by our church leaders and reflects our goals and plans for the future. It's very well done.

New: Mission is the central work required to accomplish the goal of vision. As with vision, Jesus has already defined the mission for every church. His mission definition cannot be improved upon by local boards or committees. It reads like this: "Then Jesus came to them and said, 'All authority in heaven and on earth has been given to me. Therefore go and make disciples of all nations, baptizing them in the name of the Father and of the Son and of the Holy Spirit, and teaching them to obey everything I have commanded you. And surely I am with you always, to the very end of the age'" (Matthew 28:18–20). The mission of every local church is to make disciples by teaching obedience to everything Jesus has commanded.

Old: Our basic church strategy is to get every person actively involved in the church's programs and encourage participation in one of our small Bible study groups.

New: While the biblical interpretation of Jesus' vision and mission should be the same for every church in our nation, local strategies for discipling may vary depending on members' spiritual gifts and the leading of the Holy Spirit. Focusing on the discipling mission of the church, our strategy is to inventory the spiritual gifts of each person and help them become engaged in a balanced effort of study and discipling—knowing and doing. To avoid the comfort trap of forever studying to the exclusion of simultaneously using what we already know, learning and discipling must be undertaken together and their application should begin simultaneously.

Old: Emphasize learning. Knowledge is power.

New: Emphasize wisdom, knowing and *doing* what is right.

Old: Christian growth, a series of events.

New: Christian growth, a lifetime process.

Old: We expect a great deal from our pastor. No, we don't know what his special gifts are, but he's paid enough to put in the extra time.

New: Using the excellent assessment materials available, pastors are encouraged to invest their time where their gifts are most effective in our discipling mission. Others in the church perform those pastoral functions where their gifts match unmet needs of the congregation.

Old: We all agree; our pastor doesn't do things the way we think he should. He doesn't preach the way we want him to.

New: To initiate, encourage, or participate in dissension, disorder, or factions in the church is biblically evil, wicked, and shameful. God hates such behavior.

Old: The major work of the church is evangelism.

New: The central work of the United States church is discipleship, teaching obedience to all of Jesus' commandments.

Old: Goal—a decision.

New: Goal—a disciple.

The Church at Large

Old: America, a Christian nation.

New: America, a discipling mission field.

Old: Promote ecumenism, move toward one church.

New: Promote unity in Jesus Christ—uniqueness in denominational gifts. The body is one, with many parts.

Old: Pray for revival.

New: Pray for a discipled nation.

Old: Pursue pluralism—glorification of diversity.

New: Glorify God through obedience to Jesus Christ—pursue unity of believers in the discipling mission of the church.

Old: Promote gospel proclamation.

New: The entire church should be engaged in making disciples.

Old: Vote for and elect Christians.

New: Make disciples and teach obedience to Jesus Christ. Every biblical goal (political, cultural, economic, moral, and religious) will come to pass in a discipled nation.

Old: The situation in the United States is nearly hopeless. The moral climate is potentially cataclysmic.

New: Christians must seize the moment. Ours is a magnificent opportunity to disciple our nation, building upon the proclamation victory God has so graciously given.

Old: Denominational bureaucracy is bloated and out-of-touch with biblical reality and discipling needs of the local church. Leaders tend to be religiously trendy.

New: Denominational bureaucracy needs to become downsized, decentralized, submissive to, and serving local church needs. The local church must be empowered to disciple the community.

Old: In the critical arena of spiritual warfare related to the discipling of nations, denominational leadership is naive and biblically out-of-touch with the times. Little or no assessment is provided of the nature, evidence, and scope of the horrendous spiritual conflict Satan is successfully waging for the souls of American Christians.

New: Denominational leadership thinks globally, plans nationally, and serves locally in terms of:

VISION: God's long-term goal. His kingdom will come when his will is done on earth as in heaven. We are to become an obedient and righteous people.

MISSION: Our central work, assigned by Jesus to achieve God's long-term goal, is to make disciples by teaching obedience to Jesus' commands.

STRATEGY: Organized plan to accomplish the central work of MISSION to achieve the long-term goal of VISION. In the local church we are to identify, develop, and simultaneously apply our spiritual gifts in the work of discipling our community, ever mindful that discipling is being and teaching obedience to the Bible. Denominational resources should be focused on fulfillment of biblical vision, mission, and strategy. Denominational leadership should undertake a SWOT analysis of their denominational situation related to the goal achievement plan of our heavenly Father and develop an overview assessment of the conflict between the children of the kingdom and the forces of evil.

Old: Target audience of Christian publishing, readers of 600 religious publications.

New: Target audience of Christian publishing, readers of 23,000 religious and secular publications. Ninety-seven percent of publications in the United States are secular.

TWO EXAMPLES OF PARADIGM SHIFTS

No one in has ever compared to Jesus as the supreme creator of momentous paradigm shifts. I am continually fascinated that Jesus, when embarking on the mission to establish his spiritual kingdom on earth, chose fishermen as his first kingdom builders. He did not seek out master planners in the world of commerce. Nor did he search for renowned leaders from the religious community, the most gifted scholars, or the most prolific and popular writers of the day. He chose fishermen. Perhaps he felt they were more teachable, more open to change. Certainly they had not established theological or doctrinal positions to be defended to justify their intellectualism. Do not be surprised if major changes in thinking come from the laity. Successful Christian businessmen are already beginning to apply their problem-solving gifts and creative energy to the work of advancing the kingdom.

More than a mood swing is taking place in our nation today. The dramatic shift in political thinking signaled in the November 1994 elections reveals a nation in the midst of deepening introspection. Increasingly, we are a people being prepared for discipling. As government decentralizes and returns power and responsibility to the states, Christians will be given new opportunity to respond to biblical obedience to caring for the poor, the homeless, the indigent, and the culturally deprived. Every loving service provided is an entree for the discipled to disciple. Major paradigm shifts will be required as we examine our obedience to tithing and beyond.

An article supporting the emergence of a people more open to change appeared in the December 1994 issue of *Emerging Trends* by George Gallup, Jr. In this superb piece titled "A Nation in Recovery," Mr. Gallup makes these observations: "There is a great deal of evidence—survey and other—to show that Americans are beginning to break their secular chains, that we are indeed in a period of spiritual renewal. As always, there are countervailing trends, reminding us that we are in the midst of what Charles Dickens described as "the best of times, and the worst of times." Despite the grim statistics about society, the unremitting voices of gloom and doom, and the sometimes desperate search for reasons and answers, the healing process is underway. We are, it would appear, a nation 'in recovery.'"

The Field Is the World

Paradigm realignment can come unexpectedly. A number of years ago I arrived at the Mount Hermon Conference Center in northern California late in the afternoon. It was my second Christian Writers' conference as a workshop leader, and I was concerned. This was one of the largest writer conferences in the nation. The faculty was made up of nationally known Christian writers, editors, and publishers in addition to some 200 or so conferees. *What am I doing here?* The question kept boring into my consciousness as I considered the professional competence of the faculty selected. I'm a small-town businessman from the Midwest. I'm not a writer, an editor, or a publisher. I was nervous, unsure of myself. *Does my message of proclamation victory achieved and the need for massive national discipling really come from God?* I walked over to the chapel. Inside, it was quiet and dark and I was alone. Mount Hermon is situated in a beautiful redwood forest. The chapel is an A-frame design. Behind the pulpit, from floor to ceiling are glass panels looking out onto a scene of majestic beauty. California redwoods shelter the little chapel. I slipped into one of the pews at the back and poured my heart out to the Lord. I don't remember how long I prayed in an anguish of uncertainty. Finally, when I looked up, I saw two vertical strips of stained glass framing the clear glass at the back of the chapel. On one panel were the words, "The field is the world." On the other, "The good seed are the children of the kingdom." I sat in awed silence as this profound spiritual truth penetrated my soul. I understood I was a child of the kingdom, and I was here to sow the good seed of the Great Commission. The peace of Jesus flowed through me as I embraced this new paradigm, and I've never doubted the authority of his mission since.

Operation Timothy

Our nation's morality will never be restored without major change in the lives of individual Christians. Such change must begin with a discipling love of one Christian for another. I met with the young vice president of our company for breakfast weekly for a year as we worked our way through the discipling experience of Operation Timothy. The ultimate paradigm shift occurs in Christians when they experience transition from a life of passive ineffectiveness to a life of discipling obedience, righteousness, and productivity. Dan Siadak, now president and chief operating officer of Russell Business Forms, Inc., describes his personal paradigm transition.

"I was raised in a loving, supportive family environment. We said grace before meals and went to church on Sundays. However, we never really engaged in any deep spiritual discussions. God was kind of left to the religion classes and church. I believed in God, but he wasn't a real, active part of my life. As I grew older, married, and started having children, I increasingly felt an uneasiness or restlessness, even though by man's standards my life was going along extremely well. It was kind of like the feeling you get when you know you aren't living up to your full potential. Through invitation, I began going to some luncheons sponsored by Christian Business Men's Committee (CBMC). At these meetings, men would give their testimonies of how they developed a personal relationship with Jesus and how it changed their lives. This stirred some emotions deep within me and led me to indicate interest in a program they offered called Operation Timothy. CBMC followed up with me through Jim Russell, my friend, mentor, and employer, who graciously offered to take me through the Operation Timothy Bible study.

"As we prayed together and worked through the material, my faith became alive. Scriptures began to take on meaning for me and illuminated what was going on in my life. It was like finally getting plugged into a circuit through the Holy Spirit and being utilized for our divinely intended purpose—to glorify God. I began to read the Bible and other Christian material regularly. I began to share this wonderful discovery with my wife and children, which led to their developing deeper relationships with God. I began to get involved in discipleship opportunities such as trying to set a worthy Christian example, Bible studies, our church youth group, starting a Church Writing Group, Promise Keepers, and simply engaging in spiritual discussions with individuals. Even the heart-wrenching, unexpected death of my younger sister provided the opportunity to start my brother-in-law on Operation Timothy.

"I have experienced many changes since accepting Jesus as my personal Savior. He has brought true meaning and focus to my career, ministry, and my life. I now enjoy a very active friendship with him. Throughout my days, whether at work, home, or other places, I often talk with him and ask for his advice, guidance, wisdom, and forgiveness. I also thank him for the many blessings he continues to grant me and my family. He provides me energy, strength, and discipline to move forward in my Christian walk and to resist temptations.

"I thank God that other Christians took the time and were willing to be disciples to me. It has been an eternal life-changing experience."

From decisions to *disciples*. Now that's a paradigm shift worthy of American Christians as they define their biblical mission for the twenty-first century.

CHAPTER 7

The Lambs Are Waiting, Gaunt and Hungry

RELIGIOUS PLURALISM IN the United States is a media-created myth. Yes, it exists in the sense that many religions are represented in the beliefs of a small number of Americans. No, it does not exist in the sense that the United States has a balanced presence of many religions within its population as is mistakenly and sometimes deliberately presented by the national media. Eighty-nine percent of Americans perceive themselves as Christians. Two percent are Jews. Six percent do not believe in God. The remaining three percent is made up of people representing all the other religions. Including Muslims, their numbers are so small as to be statistically unidentifiable. Religious pluralism as it is propagandized in the United States has no basis of truth, as revealed in statistical reality. By any measure of numerical majority, with 89 percent of its people perceiving themselves as Christians, the United States could be called a Christian nation. By any measure of obedience to the commandments of Jesus Christ as the Christian standard, the United States could be called a heathen nation.

THE FIELD IS RIPE FOR THE HARVEST

A majority of Christians who believe in the death and resurrection of Jesus Christ are the undiscipled lambs who are waiting, gaunt and hungry. Spiritually malnourished, weakened by the emptiness of their search for meaning in life, hollowed out by the missing values of their material and sensual fast-track, deeply sensing there is more to life, not knowing how to find it, starved for meaningful relationships, these guilt-ridden, searching lambs are everywhere around us. We stand next to them in the grocery check-out lines. They work beside us during the day. We are seated together at church. They are the unknowing victims of our irritation with traffic. Jesus is known to them primarily by the solid conviction of their belief in his life, death, resurrection, and spiritual existence. Beyond the elementary basics of their faith, which is scripturally valid and real to them, theirs is a world of biblical ignorance. While each is a member of our Christian family as defined by Jesus in John 3:16, they probably could not describe their qualifications for membership in the Christian family to the satisfaction of today's hardened, hypocritical Christian skeptic. Without discipled obedience or understanding, many have never attended nor possess a desire to attend church. More than anything in the world, they need a compassionate friend who, in sacrificial love, will teach them obedience to all Jesus has commanded; someone who will nourish them through their spiritual infancy, who will nurture them in the wonder, joy, and freedom of the Christian walk.

A state of divine euphoria should be sweeping the Christian community as it discovers the unrecognized but beckoning harvest field existing today, but only despair exists. These discipling opportunities are everywhere. They result from generations of faithful, dedicated, persistent proclamation of the Good News. Unequaled in its historic perseverance, God is rewarding the proclamation devotion of American Christians with a discipling harvest that is historically unprecedented. He waits patiently for our discipling discernment and biblical wisdom to catch up to our proclamation zeal. He waits for love to overcome the spiritual laziness of believers to be replaced by renewed energy for discipling obedience.

FEED MY LAMBS

Jesus expects us to tell others the Good News and then lead them to deepen their faith in him. He then expects those we disciple to lead others to him. Jesus illustrates this in the exchange he has with Peter after the disciples had returned from a long night of fishing. After finishing the breakfast he had prepared for them, Jesus turned to Peter and asked, "Simon, son of John, do you truly love me more than these?"

"Yes, Lord," Peter replied, "you know that I love you."

Jesus said, "Feed my lambs" (John 21:15).

THE FRANTIC SEARCH FOR MEANING IN LIFE

Never before in history have circumstances been so right to the obedience called for in this biblical vignette as do the present circumstances in the United States. A majority of Americans fall into the category of undiscipled lambs. Americans have become a people driven by two powerful undercurrents. Gallup studies show one of these dominant trends is the intensified search for meaning in life. This is accompanied by the individual desire to see their religious faith grow. A second dominant trend is an, "intensified search for deeper, more meaningful relationships, so desperately needed in our impersonal and fragmented society." Willingness to express a longing for fulfillment of these deep inner needs should be recognized by Christians as encouraging signs signaling major discipling opportunities. Since it has been established that 85 percent of Americans already believe in the life, death, resurrection, and spiritual existence of Jesus Christ, readers of this book should not be surprised that the vast majority of those expressing an intensified search for meaning in life and for meaningful relationships are already Christians. The lambs are waiting, gaunt and hungry. Are we prepared and willing to undertake the loving disciplines required to feed them? They are waiting in long lines, each with different problems, circumstances, hurts, fears, longings, and wounds to be healed. More than any other remedy, they need to be lovingly bathed in biblical truth.

A recent op-ed piece in a Lansing paper illustrates one of the problems resulting from a lack of discipline—the breakdown in relationships. Not many people are willing to lay out their hurts for everyone to see, but one woman did in a piece headlined, "No-fault Divorce Hurts Women and Children." A subtitle read, "The innocent spouse shouldn't have to pay for the other's sins." It was written by a local woman describing her own life-shattering experience. The unexpected pain and fear become real as she tells her story. "My husband of thirty years is divorcing me because he claims he isn't happy and he doesn't want to be here. We all know that is not the real reason. With no-fault divorce, you don't need a reason. You could leave a marriage now because of a hangnail. That's how much sense this all makes to me.

"I had hopes and dreams of enjoying the last years of my life with my husband, traveling and just being with him when he retired. Now I worry in terror where I'll live, about my medical insurance, life insurance, and just plain survival. I worked very hard taking care of my husband, two children, and elderly parents.

"Where are my rewards for being there for people dear to me? Where does this place me in this corrupt society? I support tougher divorce laws. It won't help me, but I'm sick of women and children being treated as second-rate citizens.

"I feel everyone deserves respect and the right to a halfway decent standard of living. Why should the innocent spouse have to pay for the other's sins? When are men and women going to stop hurting each other and the family and friends of each of them? What do our children, young and old, have to believe in nowadays when their own parents, friends, and others are destroying the family unit? It devastates everyone. What happened to our morals, our trust and commitment? ... Why should a woman have to jump into a world she doesn't feel comfortable in and feel her job as a housewife, mother, and caretaker of her parents wasn't important?

"I loved my role in life. My children never took guns to school and never took drugs and both went to college. I'm proud of my life, and yet everyone says get on with your new way of life. There wasn't anything wrong with my old life. It's only because I am thrown into a terrible situation not of my doing.

"No place in my Bible does it say because I chose to stay home I committed a sin. Since when do people have the right to judge me so badly by making me lose so much? The innocent spouse pays forever. Family, friends, and oh, yes, grandchildren are left with an empty feeling, a loss that never can be replaced by that one loved one.

"I guess it boils down to the fact that people are only worth something if they bring home a big paycheck. How sad that greed has taken over in this world. Love, trust, and commitment to others is gone.

"I guess marriage vows are empty words. If things get hard in a marriage, we can all just get a divorce.

"It's as though we can all be thrown out like yesterday's garbage."

The plight of this woman breaks my heart. Surely, an obedient Christian friend, bringing a discipling influence into the life of her spouse could have made a difference. An obedient discipling Christian in the life of the other woman alluded to could have made a difference. Were you or I, because of our discipling failure, the cause of this tragedy?

THE NEED TO RETURN TO BIBLICAL VALUES

Salt and light must be restored in American life before the deplorable ratio of divorces to marriages will improve. In the not-too-distant past, divorce was recognized as a result of shameful, socially unacceptable, biblically prohibited behavior on the part of one or both marriage partners. Sinful behavior in marriage can vary from anger to infidelity. Whatever the cause, selfishness dominating the life of one or both of those involved, is central to the problem. In the past the stigma, humiliation, and shame associated with divorce was so intense, so socially, culturally, and morally repugnant, that those prevailing attitudes and the violation of understood biblical norms served as a strong inhibiting influence on divorce. Fear of social rejection strengthened self-control and inspired solutions to marital problems tending to preserve the marriage. Christians must once again publicly define the biblical rejection and personal shame related to divorce. This is known as being a disciple and making disciples by teaching obedience to Jesus' commandments.

Characteristics respected and admired by Christians and seen as predominant strengths in a solid marriage begin with faithfulness and are reinforced by fidelity and self-control. The honor, dignity, and self-respect embodied in faithfulness were qualities one could live and die for.

Ours is a time when the character of the twentieth-century Christian male needs to again measure up to biblical standards. His first major test comes in the evaluation of his responsibility as a Christlike example as the spiritual leader of his family. When 50 percent of all marriages in the United States are ending in divorce, he obviously fails his first important leadership trial—that of being a faithful spouse, a loving father, and a discipling mentor, teaching his family obedience to God's Word. It soon becomes evident that Christian men are almost totally ignorant of their biblical calling to be spiritual role models for their family.

Men need to be challenged by the qualities of love, courage, discipline, and commitment essential to their biblical responsibility as spiritual head of the family. Men need to be inspired by the blessings of natural affection, joy, peace, and self-worth that comes in submission to Christ in the spiritual leadership of a loving family. They must understand that this responsibility is a biblical mandate! While Christian men engage peripherally in the dialogue pertaining to family values, too many of them do not understand the central role played by the spiritual quality of love in the tensions of family life. To understand the meaning of family values, you must first understand the meaning of love.

As the smallest social unit in a community and nation, the cultural, moral, and value trends of the family will determine the advance or decline of the national character. Americans should be careful not to minimize the critical importance of an intensified national focus on family values. Love is the unifying power and central quality essential to a healthy family. Stable families are the foundation upon which, great nations grow and are enabled to bring a positive influence upon the worldwide family of nations. What are the individual responsibilities in a healthy family? How can love be defined?

Among the most wonderful things a father can do for his children is to love their mother. Openly cherishing and treating the mother with dignity and respect is an example of fatherly love that will forever shape the lives and future families of the children. The father role model does not require an ego-driven image of macho superiority, nor the endless pursuit of the vanity of intellectualism. A profound difference exists between the vanity of intellectualism and the pursuit of knowledge leading to biblical wisdom. Rather, the father should teach a hunger for wisdom, the biblical definition of which is "knowing and doing what is right." As role model, fathers are to be in submissive obedience to their heavenly Father. The Bible always is the contemporary home-study course. The discipling role model begins at home. First lambs to be fed are those in our immediate family.

Addressing the role of wife and mother, prize-winning author Dr. Mary Ann Diorio says, "As a woman, I have the magnificent privilege of being on the cutting edge of history because of my high calling to be the 'maker of a home.' When the woman fails to function as the heart, the family will fall and the nation will soon follow." She further states, "The woman has been given the awesome responsibility of planting and cultivating the seeds of peace through the unfailing power of love . . . in her love, she comes most closely to resembling God."

Obedience is the primary responsibility of children. In his New Testament letter to the Ephesians, Paul said, "Children, obey your parents. This is the right thing to do because God has placed them over you. If you honor your father and mother, yours will be a long life full of blessing" (Ephesians 6:1–2).

Today, the greatest fear of teenagers is not poverty, or scholastic failure, or nuclear war; it is losing one or both of their parents. Tragically, more than 50 percent of all children in the United States will live through their greatest fear before they are eighteen.

To understand family values, you must know the meaning of love. Love is understood when a person knows the inner self. You cannot know yourself without an intimate knowledge of God, your Creator. God reveals the meaning of love in his Word, "Love is very patient and kind, never jealous or envious, never boastful or proud, never haughty or selfish or rude. Love does not demand its own way. It is not irritable or touchy. It does not hold grudges and will hardly even notice when others do it wrong. It is never glad about injustice, but rejoices whenever truth wins out. If you love someone, you will be loyal to him no matter what the cost, you will always believe in him, always expect the best of him, always stand your ground in defending him. All the special gifts and powers from God will someday come to an end, but love goes on forever" (1 Corinthians 13:4–8 TLB).

Understanding of and obedience to the biblical definition of love will bring healing to hurting families, change the character of the American people, and reverse the moral and spiritual decline of our nation. Spiritual restoration of the divine institution of marriage and family life will be among the early, great blessings of a discipled nation. The lambs are waiting, gaunt and hungry.

DISCIPLING IN ACTION: A CASE STUDY

He was in his early twenties when he served in the Vietnam War. His exemplary courage earned him four Bronze Stars, three for valor in battle. Twenty years later, his life was a mess. Alcoholism had taken its toll. Divorce ended his prewar first marriage and custody of his son went to his former wife. He became involved in a turbulent live-in relationship with his most recent female friend. She had a daughter in her early teens who also lived at home. I prayed for him from time to time. Then one day early in 1992, I asked him if he would be interested in meeting with me regularly to study the Bible. Somewhat to my surprise, he said he would like to. He lived about forty miles away. His business brought him through Lansing from time to time. We were able to meet quite regularly and began working our way through Book One of the Operation Timothy discipling manual.

This easy-to-use study guide is divided into six chapters. They are: (1) How to Know You Have Eternal Life, (2) How to Understand the Work of Christ, (3) How to Be Sure of God's Deliverance, (4) How to Experience God's Forgiveness, (5) How to Love by the Power of the Holy Spirit, and (6) How to Communicate with God.

As the weeks and months passed, he saw that the power of God's truth was bringing fresh conviction into his life regarding personal accountability for right and wrong behavior. Heightened concern for the welfare of the teenage daughter and the immoral example presented by his live-in relationship with her mother was difficult to reconcile with his new understanding of God's expectations of him. At each of our meetings we prayed through the problems in our lives and always with the implicit understanding that ultimately we must bring our lives into obedience and harmony with biblical truth. While his problems were more severe than mine, I never took the position that he had problems and I did not. Self-righteousness is a major albatross inhibiting Christian effectiveness today. Finally, he said his good-byes, ending the immoral relationship he was in, not without sorrow, hurt, and sadness for all involved.

Yesterday, three years later, I met with him to discuss the impact of God in his life. Happily married for nearly three years, he attends church faithfully and takes children in the neighborhood to Sunday school each week. We talked for almost two hours. He described how he always knew he was a Christian. He believed in the life, death, resurrection, and spiritual presence of Jesus Christ. His basic faith and understanding carried him through the Vietnam War. In battle he always prayed for protection. He knew that if he was blown up, he would be in heaven. He never worried or had any doubt about where he would go. Men were killed and wounded on either side. He always prayed with believing faith. God never failed him.

Then, with tears in his eyes, he volunteered the information that caused me to catch my breath as he confirmed what I suspected deep in my heart. He said, "Uncle Jim, one of the biggest days of my life was the day you called and showed that someone cared enough for me to want to work with me and teach me about the Bible." Then he thoughtfully added, "That was probably the most special day I ever had." I blinked back the stinging tears, and we sat in silence as God's love rolled over us and we basked in the discipling fruitfulness of that precious moment. He had been a waiting lamb, gaunt and hungry. Jesus said, "Peter, do you really love me? Feed my lambs."

Eric continued, "Operation Timothy was the opening of my mind to the things of God and the desire to learn and obey more of the truth. Those like me who know practically nothing need someone to take the time to teach us the meaning of biblical truth." Jesus said, "Make disciples . . . by teaching them to obey everything I have commanded you."

God is easily capable of discipling our nation. He chooses to do it through those whose faith assures them he is easily capable. He waits while the numbers grow. He waits for Christians to be captured by his vision, by Christ's mission, and by the strategic, entrepreneurial leading of the Holy Spirit. Understanding of the enlarged vision of our heavenly Father will emerge from a tightened focus on the discipling mission mandate of Jesus Christ as defined in Matthew 28:18–20. At this point, it may be wise to study how we can become effective and productive in our knowledge of Jesus Christ through discipling obedience.

How Can I Be Discipled?

1. Read at least one chapter of God's Word every day with a mind totally open to the Holy Spirit's revelation of truth. Hold no defensive positions.

2. Be accountable in an intimate Bible study group. Participate for the specific purpose of becoming effective and productive in the knowledge of your discipling mission.

3. Listen prayerfully to your pastor's lessons every Sunday. You may learn biblical truth that is present but unrecognized by even the pastor.

4. Pray for God to bring into your awareness and possession those books and articles he wants you to read.

5. Acquire and build your own cassette tape library so you can be discipled as you drive your car.

6. Be engaged in the one-on-one discipling of at least one other person. You will be surprised at how you are discipled in the loving act of teaching obedience to another.

7. Submit yourself in a tutoring relationship with a respected biblical mentor.

Discipling Your Family

1. Faithfully pray before every meal, thanking God for his food and asking him to bless it.

2. Pray together during any family crisis. Pray regularly as a family in praise and thanksgiving.

3. Be the example you proclaim.

4. Be faithful in the application of personal integrity.

5. Read the Bible daily and teach its truths and principles in timely response to the tensions and problems of everyday life.

6. Be bold in your witness and discipling.

7. Give generously and cheerfully.

8. Lift up and teach the qualities of the "fruit of the spirit" in family relations. They are love, joy, peace, patience, kindness, goodness, faithfulness, gentleness, and self-control.

Discipling in Public, or Being Identifiably Christian in the Culture

1. Whenever dining out with Christians, always give thanks and ask God's blessing on the food.

2. Engage in discipling witness with sensitivity, faith, and courage.

3. Use all available public forums for teaching obedience. Form a church writing group. Write letters to the editor, op-ed pieces, guest editorials, and book reviews of good Christian books. Reinforce your writing with the biblical authority of Scripture.

4. Be alert for opportunities to loan or give discipling books, cassette tapes, and Christian magazines to those you meet

casually, such as gas station attendants, customer service people, and public servants.

5. Seek opportunities to serve on your local school board, library committee, or the advisory panel of your local newspaper. Be lovingly Christian, not confrontational or adversarial. Manifest the fruit of the Holy Spirit.

6. Participate in local talk-radio. Apply biblical truth to the issues of the day.

7. Participate in local public-access television. Most need a biblical worldview perspective.

8. Rule-of-thumb guidelines for effectively addressing current issues from a Christian perspective might be these five considerations: (a) Identify an issue headlining the daily news. (b) Define the issue for the reading, listening, or viewing audience. (c) Apply biblical truth, biblical principle to the issue. (d) Reinforce it with Scripture. (e) Close it in love. God may hate the behavior, but he always loves the individual.

Discipling Others One-on-One

1. If God has not identified the next person, or the first person, with whom you are to be engaged in discipling, ask him. Surely, that request must be among the sweetest prayers he hears.

2. Discipling one-on-one is always preceded by compassionate prayer that Christ's love will be the central agent and power of communication.

3. When discipling, I readily acknowledge it when I don't have an answer. My attitude is always one of joy that we will learn this together as we begin a search of reference material. I try to have a concordance, at least one parallel Bible, and a dictionary present.

4. Each meeting is opened with prayer. If I sense this spiritual infant is uncomfortable and not ready to pray audibly by himself, I never press the issue, but rather, assure him that when

he is ready in later meetings, he can do so. I then open and close with prayer. Every third or fourth meeting, I offer the opportunity. Every person I've ever discipled has become comfortable in audible prayer before we've completed the first study-guide book.

5. I find the best length of time for such discipling meetings will be from seventy-five to ninety minutes. This seems the most appropriate for an evening meeting. If the meeting is at lunch or some other time of day, then it may need to be shortened.

6. The Operation Timothy book-one study guide is so designed that the one being discipled sets the pace for the progress made as they read the questions and then find the answers in the Bible. Discussion takes place in the analysis of the scriptural answer.

The above lists are obviously only starting ideas, intended to help you in shaping your discipling agenda.

Every Christian must have a sense of the mission importance of his or her discipling contribution to the grandest cause in all of human history, that of discipling our nation in obedience to the Great Commission mandate of our Lord Jesus Christ. This discipling mandate is the ultimate expression of loving obedience called for in the Great Commandment. Here Jesus said, "Love the lord your God with all your heart and with all your soul and with all your mind. This is the first and greatest commandment. And the second is like it: Love your neighbor as yourself" (Matthew 22:37–38). Can there be a higher form of love than that in which we make a disciple by teaching obedience of all Jesus has commanded us? Jesus said, "Feed my lambs." The lambs are waiting, gaunt and hungry. Our response must be, "Here I am, Lord, I will go!"

CHAPTER 8

The Amy Foundation—
Discipling Initiatives

AS OUR FAMILY doctor approached, I was immediately aware of the concern in his eyes and the frown replacing his normal smile. Without waiting for me to speak, he said, "Phyllis is doing fine, and you have a little girl, but we have a problem with the baby."

"What's that?" I asked, feeling relieved and anxious at the same time.

"The baby is a Mongoloid," he answered.

My stomach tightened as my mind expanded to take in the horrendous implications of that fearful term. "Oh, no!" I half-whispered. I was remembering the imbecilic boy of our neighbors when I was a child. Although he was nine, he remained a two-year-old mentally. He, too, was called a Mongoloid. He couldn't speak and would stand for hours in a corner, watching a piece of string he twirled as he drooled continuously. My heart instantly grieved for Phyllis.

"Does Phyllis know?" I asked.

"No," he responded. "We thought you might want to tell her after she has the baby home for a week or two."

My next concern became what additional care would be required for Amy over the first few years of her life. We had agreed that if our fifth child was a girl, we would name her Amy, which we knew meant "beloved." Before long, we realized how meaningful that term was regarding Amy. The doctor said Amy would have serious respiratory problems. She would be difficult to toilet train. She might be seven before that could be achieved. There could be serious heart problems. She wouldn't walk before two or three years. Amy would have small ears, a protruding tongue, inclined eyes, reduced thumb-size, she may be double-jointed, and definitely mentally handicapped. Amy was missing a single chromosome. Today, her condition is known as Down's Syndrome.

I couldn't bring myself to tell Phyllis about Amy for nearly a month. She was scheduled to take the baby in for her first check-up the next day. That evening, I knew the time had arrived. I told her our baby had serious problems, that she was Down's Syndrome, and I described some of the prognosis implications. Phyllis was crushed. She found it difficult to believe because Amy was so beautiful and such a good baby. As I comforted her, I told her that, as Christians, I believed our response must be God-honoring and in perfect harmony with biblical truth. I had two specific passages of Scripture in mind that I believed should govern our attitudes and behavior and should reign over our grief. They were, "give thanks in all circumstances, for this is God's will for you in Christ Jesus" (1 Thessalonians 5:18). The second, which I felt important, was, "And we know that in all things God works for the good of those who love him, who have been called according to His purpose" (Romans 8:28). So Phyllis and I thanked God for Amy just the way she was, and we assured him we loved her just the way she was. I didn't tell Phyllis that during her pregnancy I had asked God to send us a child that would have an impact for him around the world. Nor did I have any inkling that he would answer that prayer in a beautiful and marvelous way.

Over the next few weeks, one by one we told our other four children about Amy. They are Kathy, who was nineteen at the time; Vicki, sixteen; Lori, ten; and Jimmy, seven. When all of our family knew about Amy, we gathered in prayer and again thanked God for Amy just the way she was and assured him we loved her just the way she was. The blessings of God through Amy began to pour into our family.

Through the love and patience of Lori, Amy was toilet trained before she was two. Kathy was protective and the finest of all baby-sitters. Vicki kept everything tidy and neat around Amy. Jimmy's love for her was natural and boyish. Amy didn't have a cold until she was nearly three. She walked rather late, around age two and a half. She required fewer visits to the doctor than any of our other children. Amy brought into our home and family a higher manifestation of the fruit of the Holy Spirit than any person I have ever known. The aura and personality of Amy is the embodiment of love, joy, peace, patience, kindness, goodness, faithfulness, gentleness, and self-control. Amy is now twenty-six, a self-assured, poised, and lovely young lady. Next month, June 1995, Amy will receive her earned high school diploma.

THE BIRTH OF THE AMY AWARDS

Last week, before nearly a thousand people attending the annual Michigan Prayer Breakfast, I presented the 1994 Amy Writing Awards $10,000 first prize to the winning author. The presentation read like this:

> "Today, May 25, 1995, and every day for the foreseeable future, several hundred thousand, and on some days millions of people across our nation will read biblical truth, reinforced with Scripture, in secular non-religious publications. This will happen because of two

national projects of the Amy Foundation, and it will take place in response to the inspiration of God's promise that His word will not return to Him void, but will accomplish the purpose for which it is sent.

"Now in its eleventh year, and acclaimed as the most popular journalism contest in the nation, the Amy Writing Awards attracts more than a thousand qualified submissions annually. These entries appear in such notable publications as the *Wall Street Journal, The Washington Post, Newsweek, U.S. News and World Report, The Atlantic,* and others of more obscure renown such as *The Catawba Valley Neighbor,* and *The Beaver Creek News Current.*

"The Amy Writing Awards program is designed to recognize creative, skillful writing that presents in a sensitive, thought-provoking manner the biblical position on issues affecting the world today. To be eligible, submitted articles must be published in a secular, nonreligious publication and must decisively quote the Word of God. When submissions arrive in our Lansing office, the name of the author and the name of the publication are removed, and each entry is assigned a number. All scoring and judging is done strictly on the merit of the text. The entire process is bathed in prayer. Increasingly, we see strong evidence of a conscious effort by key editorial executives of secular print media to improve their religious coverage. There is a new openness to thoughtful Christian commentary and complaints of Scripture deletion because of editorial narrowness are becoming rare. Discipling progress is being made, and God is preparing an unprecedented opportunity for Christian discipling."

AMY AWARDS STILL IMPACTING LIVES

Life experience has shown me what God will do through ordinary people the seemingly impossible acts when they act in faith, obedience, and love and in harmony with his Word. Over many years, I had become increasingly distressed by the absence of a biblical perspective in the news coverage of major media outlets. Christians seemed to have totally abandoned the idea of and discipling responsibility for articulation of biblical world-view in secular radio, television, and print media. Finally, in 1984, Phyllis and I were preparing for our first extended Florida vacation, and I said to her, "Nobody seems to be picking up on this problem. It looks to me as though Christians have deserted secular-print media and retreated into a psychological ghetto of cultural isolation. I am so tormented by this problem that it looks like I will have to do something myself." I purchased a typewriter with the idea I would write two or three articles dealing with issues headlining the daily news. They would be written from a biblical perspective, and I'd attempt to get them published upon our return from Florida.

Here is where God stepped in. With my act of faith in purchasing the typewriter and my determination to write in discipling obedience, God did a wonderful thing. From the moment we arrived in Florida, he began to show me there was a superior way to accomplish the goal, and he was prepared to honor a larger vision. Not a single sheet of paper entered the typewriter. In his loving graciousness, he began to shape every major aspect of the Amy Writing Awards in my mind. Before we left Florida, the structure, the incentives, and promotion were organized and ready for final planning and implementation. Upon our return to Lansing, the Amy Foundation committee was formed, and the 1985 Amy Writing Awards program was launched.

Today, instead of my writing a few obscure pieces, over a thousand articles presenting biblical truth, reinforced with Scripture, are published annually across the nation. They are published in secular, nonreligious publications. The Amy Writing Awards is not only an encouragement to Christian writers, but the high quality of the prize-winning essays establishes a fresh credibility for biblical truth in the mind of the skeptic. Each year the Amy Foundation publishes a booklet containing the fifteen prize-winning entries. It is mailed without charge to 34,000 people on our mailing list. The list is a cross-section of journalists and includes the editor of each of the 2000 daily newspapers in the United States. Department heads of 800 college-level English and Journalism departments are on the list. Eighteen thousand past subscribers to *Quill* magazine receive it as well. Every person submitting an entry or inquiring for information is added. A discipling strategy is at work in this process because we are convinced professional pride and curiosity will compel every writer to read at least the entry that earned a fellow journalist or author a check for $10,000. Each article is required to include at least one passage of Scripture, because we are depending on God's promise that his Word will not return to him void but will accomplish the purpose for which it is sent. It follows that every person who reads a qualified Amy entry is exposed to a discipling experience.

Entries for the Amy Writing Awards and inquiries for information pertaining to the other work of the Amy Foundation arrive from around the world. They come from Pakistan, Taiwan, Japan, Ethiopia, Nigeria, Ireland, and many other nations.

We serve a prayer-answering God. Amy's life is having a discipling impact worldwide. God has answered my secret prayer beyond my expectations.

The ten-year national success of the Amy Writing Awards establishes a breakthrough opportunity for Christian professional, freelance, and latent writers in the church to present biblical truth reinforced with Scripture in secular, nonreligious publications. Ten annual Amy booklets containing the prize-winning articles for the years from 1985 through 1994 lay to rest forever the satanic myth that Christians cannot publish biblical truth containing Scripture in secular nonreligious publications. Only lack of faith, lack of courage, lack of obedience, lack of righteousness, lack of love, and lack of discipling vision and effort, stands in our way today. There are no remaining valid, external excuses preventing Christians from discipling our nation through local and national print media.

Less than thirty days after I had presented the biblical discipling vision, mission, and strategy defined by the ministries of the Amy Foundation at the Florida Christian Writers conference in January 1994, I received the following letter from one of the conferees. He headed up the media department for one of the space program suppliers at Cape Kennedy.

Dear Jim,

It works! Please be encouraged by the enclosed as you are in no small part to blame, due to your obedience to the Holy Spirit.

Please be convinced (re-convinced, encouraged?) by your efforts and resources in attending things like the Florida Christian Writers Conference. It is worth it! Certainly I never would have believed I could quote as much Scripture as I did here and get it published in the local, secular weekly! This is done by Gannet and inserted in the largest daily in the area, *Florida Today*.

May he continue to bless your ministry,

Here is another letter from Beaumont Texas:

The Amy Foundation Writing Awards

Dear Editors:

After hearing of Jim Russell's mission last October, and having written a newspaper column since 1977 for the very purpose of reaching out, teaching and "discipling" Christians, I was eager to see how supportive my editors would be of such a bold and blatant effort as direct quotation of the Bible in secular media.

I am thrilled and amazed anew, although I really shouldn't be, at how smoothly our efforts glide when the Spirit ushers them along! With the encouragement of Mr. Russell and with the zeal of Bob Briner's lively metaphor, I roared, without a tad of anxiety, embarrassment, or any hesitation.

I have also received many letters and calls from persons who read, and were indeed "discipled" by these articles, for which I am humbly joyful and thankful to be a part.

Most important, we have also begun a new Christian Writers' Group according to the outline materials sent from the Amy Foundation. Please include us in your prayers as we do you in ours.

My sincere gratitude is sent to each of you who inspire, exhort, and support the energies of Christian writers and writing Christians.

Thank you ..."

The Amy Writing Awards is an effective effort to open the hearts of the gatekeepers of the culture and prepare the way for Christians to present biblical truth to the nation in a discipling, obedient response. Should this not be recognized as the central work for every individual Christian and Christian church in the United States?

CHURCH WRITING GROUP MOVEMENT

The Church Writing Group movement is a discipling strategy. Possessing phenomenal numerical promise, its potential contribution to the discipling of our nation is mind-boggling. It holds the epitome of Christian effectiveness and productivity as outlined by Peter in 2 Peter 1:5–9. Remember our definitions of Vision, Mission, and Strategy. As a strategy, the Church Writing Group movement is an organized plan to do the central work of Mission, to achieve the goal of Vision. Remember, the central work of Mission is to make disciples by teaching obedience to everything Jesus has commanded us.

While not a substitute for one-on-one discipling, the CWG movement is a culture shaping, climate enhancing, dialogue building, Bible teaching, community-wide, church building, discipling labor of Christ-centered love. The Church Writing Group movement is a call to the latent writers in the Christian Church to come forth. It is Holy Spirit inspired, led, organized, and empowered. It is made up of homemakers, accountants, plumbers, physicians, salesmen, taxi-drivers, school teachers, and painters. Effectiveness of this movement proceeds from the valid premise that if you can write a letter to a friend, you can write a discipling letter to the editor! Our heavenly Father blesses the day of small beginnings.

THE POSSIBILITIES ARE STAGGERING

Local print media is an important grassroots channel for this discipling. Reader surveys show that 60–80 percent of newspaper readers read letters to the editor. They are the second most popular feature in the newspaper, second only to the obituaries. Additionally, op-ed pieces, guest editorials, book-review opportunities, and other discipling possibilities exist. If only 3 percent of America's Christian churches form a Church Writing Group to teach obedience through the local secular media, we will have 10,500 groups across the nation. Keep in mind there are only 2000 daily newspapers in the United States. If each Church Writing Group commits itself to publishing just two discipling articles per month (too modest a goal), reinforced with a passage of Scripture, that becomes 252,000 messages per year. When multiplied by the circulation of each publication, the discipling reach-out becomes incredible. Thousands of articles in millions of circulation copies will result in megamillions of reader-discipling experiences across the nation every year!

Such enormous scriptural exposure, strengthened by the biblical promise that God's Word will not return to him void but will accomplish the purpose for which it is sent (Isaiah 55:11) can support an awakening of obedience to the national discipling mandate called for by our Lord in the Great Commission (Matthew 28:18–20). The Church Writing Group movement provides each church an opportunity to biblically influence the spiritual character of the local community.

An example of the CWG discipling effectiveness can be seen in the experience of our small church in Lansing, Michigan. The *Lansing State Journal* has a daily circulation of 72,000 and a Sunday circulation of 95,000. Considering that 60–80 percent of readers read letters to the editor, when a member of the Bretton Woods Covenant Church CWG publishes a discipling letter to the editor, reinforced with Scripture, we have, in effect, added 43,000 participants to our weekly Bible study. When such a discipling letter to the editor is published in the Sunday edition of the *Lansing State Journal*, we have in effect added 57,000 participants to our adult Sunday school class. Since reader surveys also show that two-and-a-half people read each paper, the numbers are even more conservative. During the first six months of CWG meetings at our church, our little group had thirteen discipling letters and op-ed pieces published. Using the most conservative numbers, in that six-month period, our CWG generated over 600,000 reader-discipling experiences. Not bad for a small church where Sunday attendance is normally less than 100. Imagine the result in ten years if 10 percent to 20 percent of the 350,000 churches in the United States caught the vision of this discipling bonanza.

Pen & Sword, a bimonthly newsletter published by the Amy Foundation, is made available without charge to those interested in starting or participating in a CWG. Through this umbilical cord of communication, we teach that the local print media is not seen as an adversary to be confronted but rather as a potential ally to be prayerfully cultivated. In our local CWG, we keep a list of all the editorial and reporting staff of the local paper, and we pray for them individually by name at each of our meetings. In less than three years there has been a noticeable change in the character of our local newspaper.

Discipleship through writing has an honorable history. The apostle Paul discipled through writing. Paul was a tentmaker, not a writer. Matthew was a tax collector, not a writer. Luke was a physician, not a writer. Peter, James and John were fishermen, not writers. These men of God, whose writings continue to disciple millions around the world today, were the latent writers in the early church.

HOW TO START A CHURCH WRITING GROUP

1. Begin now to pray for your group and for the letters, articles, and columns to be written. Commit your efforts to fulfilling His Great Commission: "make disciples . . . teach obedience . . ."

2. Enlist the interest and support of the pastors and lay leaders in your church. Offer to present the CWG vision briefly in a meeting or worship service. Show the CWG video.

3. Gather a core of five or more interested people. Share the Amy brochures and newsletters with as many as possible and encourage their participation.

4. Personally invite as many as possible to a first meeting. Announce meetings in the church bulletin and at the Sunday worship service. Adopt Matthew 28:18–20 as your statement of purpose. Your mission is to "make disciples," using the secular-print media. The message: "Teach them to obey everything I have commanded you."

5. Schedule monthly meetings or more often if desired. Secure group commitment to one published piece per month minimum, with individual commitment of one piece per quarter from each participant.

6. Celebrate your victories! Recently published authors should share their experience, new insights, strategies, and so forth. Recently published authors are celebrities of the meeting. While we celebrate individual success, we give the credit and glory to God.

7. Remember, 60–80 percent of newspaper subscribers read letters to the editor, and at least two people read most subscriptions. Rejoice in the size of the audience being reached. Keep a record of the number of reader-discipling experiences achieved.

8. Eighty-nine percent of Americans perceive themselves as Christians. Eighty-five percent believe in the divinity of Jesus Christ. Seventy-four percent profess a commitment. Your reading audience is part of our family needing discipling. Teach them to be obedient to all that Jesus has commanded. Two or three discipling paragraphs reinforced with Scripture can become a life-changing experience to the reader.

9. Identify a group leader or facilitator with a heart for the vision of the Great Commission and CWG movement. Support that person with your prayers, presence, and active participation.

10. Network with other Church Writing Groups in your area. Plan common gatherings to share victories, enthusiasm, and ideas. Pray for other Church Writing Groups in your community and help them get started. The local goal is a minimum of one discipling letter to the editor each day. Nationally, our goal is at least one discipling letter to the editor every day in every newspaper in every city across our nation. Our discipling target is for that goal to be reached by the year 2001. Beginning now, we should praise God at every CWG meeting, giving him the glory for the victory he has already given us in our mighty Lord and Savior, Jesus Christ, the King of kings and Lord of lords.

CHURCH WRITING GROUP CHARACTERISTICS AND GUIDELINES

- The major purpose is to disciple readers through the secular-print media. Our goal is to teach obedience to everything Jesus has commanded us.
- Because 85 percent of Americans believe in the divinity of Jesus Christ and 74 percent confess commitment to him, the secular-reading audience should be recognized as family, as spiritual infants, as the lambs of whom Jesus said, "Peter, do you really love me? Feed my lambs."
- The writing language will be contemporary secular English, not "fluent evangelical" or "fellowship Christianese."
- Church Writing Group meetings will be bathed in prayer. The communication power is God's love for all his children.

- Regular, faithful Bible study by each writer is essential to success.
- The writing should never be strident or harsh, making simple points with sledgehammers. This only embarrasses the body of Christ.
- The writing will clearly and compassionately teach obedience to the commandments of Jesus and reflect the fruits of the spirit: love, joy, peace, patience, kindness, goodness, faithfulness, gentleness, and self-control. These should be embodied in the spiritual character of the author.
- CWG participants will meet on a scheduled, regular basis. There should be group commitment to a minimum of one published piece per month.
- Critical to the CWG mission, each published work should contain at least one passage of Scripture. It should be carefully woven into the text, identified as biblical, and reinforce the Christ-centered truth being taught.
- Sensitive, appropriate use of Scripture is required. It calls forth the power of the promise of God, that his Word will not return to him void but will accomplish the purpose for which it is sent.
- Sound research is valued. Group members share resources and ideas.
- Writing projects are discussed, critiqued, and strengthened by group review. Encouragement rather than harsh criticism is vital.
- CWG members will strive to be well-informed about current events of a local, regional, national, and global nature.
- Biblical positions regarding social, moral, and cultural conflicts should be determined and communicated.

- Church Writing Group participants will strengthen their talents through Christian writer conferences, publications, and correspondence courses.
- Participants will read broadly from both Christian and secular authors, publications, and resources so their writing reflects understanding of diverse views, adding power and credibility to their biblical perspective.
- Writers will participate in one-on-one discipling to experience growth, obedience, and teaching.
- Well-designed, widely used discipling materials will be studied and principles understood to enhance discipling through writing skills and techniques. Carl F. H. Henry points out in his book, *Twilight of a Great Civilization* that we should devote more time exhibiting the superiority of the biblical worldview and proclaiming the victories of the gospel than in exposing the vanities of our generation.
- Church Writing Groups within the church will energize the body of Christ spiritually and mobilize resources in harmony with the will of God. Print-media employees will be influenced as they read the compelling, biblical positions of Spirit-led Christian writers. Print-media readers will be discipled. The mandate of the Great Commission of our Lord Jesus Christ will be fulfilled in obedience and love.

Increasingly, we see strong evidence of a conscious effort by key editorial executives of secular-print media to improve their religious coverage. A new openness to thoughtful Christian commentary and complaints of Scripture deletion because of editorial narrowness are becoming rare. Discipling progress is being made, and God is preparing an unprecedented discipling opportunity for professional, freelance, and emerging latent writers possessing the discernment of biblical vision to communicate these truths in a unity of mission leading to the discipling of America.

Every Christian should pray every day for a discipled nation in this generation!

CHAPTER 9

Discipling Strategies—Print Media, Radio, and Television

AHUGE, DIVERSIFIED audience, generating thirty billion dollars in advertising revenues from business and industry is available to discipling Christians at no cost.

Publishing statistics report 84 percent of persons over eighteen read newspapers. United States' census results establish the presence of more than 190 million adults over eighteen. This translates into a newspaper-reading audience of nearly 160 million. No wonder the newspaper industry competes so well against radio and television. Ink on paper has staying power not possessed by its major competitors. Long after the thirty-second sound byte from radio or television has faded into oblivion, the morning or evening newspaper is waiting on the sofa or kitchen table to capture a second or third reader's attention by the power of the advertiser's persuasive appeal.

Community access features of the local newspaper are among its most popular and widely read attractions. Letters to the editor, read by 60 percent to 80 percent of their reading audience, places this favored forum in the category of "Greatest missed discipling opportunity of the century." Next is the op-ed section, or opinion-editorial possibilities, normally positioned opposite the editorial page. Here the discerning Christian can teach biblical truth with more freedom, since op-ed pieces can normally be several hundred words long. In Lansing, local editors prefer approximately 600 words for these short essays. At a more advanced level are the guest editorials. As writing skills develop and the writer becomes known by the editors as one who provides thoughtful commentary of biblical truth in a reasoned and persuasive style, their work is seen as making an important contribution to the public dialogue. Building a credible reputation opens the way for guest editorials.

One of the most overlooked windows of discipling communication are book reviews in the local newspaper. Beyond the very specific book review offerings appearing regularly is the letter to the editor that presents a fascinating vignette from an instructive Christian book and then works in the title and author's name for the reader's benefit. Suburban weeklies are especially open and always looking for well-written work from local residents.

With 350,000 Christian churches in the United States and 150 million members, no valid reason exists why the Christian community through the Church Writing Group Movement cannot present one discipling piece per day in each of the 11,600 newspapers in the United States. Of these 11,000-plus publications, 1,780 are daily, 8,540 are weekly, and 570 are semiweekly. Christians, here available to you at no cost except your discipling love, exist the resources of a communications industry employing 428,000 people with a payroll of ten billion dollars. Is there any reason or excuse acceptable to Jesus for the continued inertia, short-sightedness, lack of innovation and imagination by the laity, clergy, and denominational leadership for our ongoing failure to use this incredible, obedience-teaching national resource? Jesus commanded us to disciple our nation. Surely Jesus would not command us to undertake an impossible assignment. Our discipling attitude should always be, Here am I, Lord, send me! Here we are, Lord, send us!

NEWS ORGANIZATIONS—OPEN TO RELIGION?

An important and timely paradigm shift is taking place in the newspaper industry today. This attitude change beckons a new era of discipling obedience. It is perfectly timed for an epochal transition of American Christians from proclaiming to discipling. It calls for disciplined focus on transition to the mission of making disciples by teaching obedience to everything Jesus has commanded us, building upon the magnificent proclamation victory that God has so graciously given.

"A surge of interest among American news organizations in improving religion coverage," announced the Religion News Service report of May 31, 1995. It outlined new challenges facing the increasing number of reporters being assigned to what is somewhat irreverently called the *"God beat."* Focusing on the new *Deities & Deadlines* by John Dart, which the report calls, "a compact primer for religion journalists," RNS describes the changing perspectives of journalism toward covering religion in America. "What some journalists affectionately call 'the God beat' includes all those otherworldly realms where many journalists, much less angels, fear to tread," says Dart, who has covered religion for the *Times* since 1967.

"Moreover, because deities, supernatural realms and miracles are unverifiable, scientifically, and journalistically, the reporter's task is to describe supernatural claims fairly and intelligently to believer and nonbeliever alike," he says. "This primer is designed to help new religion reporters get a faster start toward impressive, balanced, and sophisticated stories."

RNS goes on. "Though fair, accurate and insightful religion reporting has been a mainstay of the 50 or so major newspapers with full-time religion writers, many of the nation's news organizations have given scant attention to religion, beyond the pieties of the Saturday church page. But as religion increasingly

is entwined with politics and public policy—and is at the root of
numerous armed conflicts—a working knowledge of the way
faith shapes human behavior is becoming essential for all kinds
of reportage.

"Recent studies—including the landmark 1993 Freedom
Forum study *Bridging the Gap, Religion and the News Media*, co-
authored by Dart and Southern Baptist leader Jimmy Allen—
prompted many newspapers and broadcast organizations to
resolve to get smarter and more sophisticated about religion
coverage.

"News organizations have begun to enhance their religion
coverage, often expanding to include ethics, spirituality, and
moral issues. ABC News has hired a full-time religion reporter;
National Public Radio and the Voice of America have added religion to their news mix; following the lead of other papers, the
Dallas Morning News recently launched a new section devoted to
religion. And stories with religion angles are increasingly land-
ing on page one or are featured on local and network news.

"Even seasoned reporters who pride themselves on being
able to explain the most complicated subjects can face new challenges when placed on the religion beat.

"Consider the simple question of Bibles. With hundreds of
versions, translations, and annotations available depending on
the denomination, which version of Scripture is appropriate for
journalism?

"Of the various Bible translations, the New Revised Standard Version and the New International Version are considered
excellent,' Dart writes. 'The King James Version is good if you
need a translation in Old English for effect, but to use the KJV
consistently is to cast today's religion in an outdated stereotype.

"What makes the religion beat so extraordinary in Dart's
view is the virtually infinite time span involved. The past matters.

And the future is crucial—especially when you're dealing with belief in the afterlife or the coming of a messiah.

"'No other news beat calls for so much use of historical background to explain current disputes, ' he writes. 'Sacred writings, myths, and events of yesteryear—as variously interpreted—are central to some religion news stories.'"

The RNS report concludes with the observation that as in all other beats their are some, "wackos." "Consider the clever *L. A. Times* copy clerk confronted in the lobby by someone who said he had an important religion story. 'You may not believe this, but I am the Messiah,' the visitor said. The clerk replied, 'You may not believe this, but you're the third one today.'"

The above represent a major change of attitudes and a significant paradigm shift in the newsrooms and editorial offices of the newspaper industry. At the Amy Foundation we see a new openness to thoughtful Christian commentary, and complaints of Scripture deletion because of editorial narrowness are rare.

Influential laity, clergy, and denominational leadership must become acutely aware that American Christians are ill-prepared for such windows of discipling opportunity. Important also, it should be recognized, such favorable circumstances last for only a short time. Christian weaknesses are seen as biblical illiteracy and lack of focus on the person and commandments of Jesus Christ. Further, Christian effectiveness is undermined by a universal ignorance of the Vision of God, the Mission assigned to all believers by Jesus, and failure to understand the need for discipling strategies such as organized plans locally to accomplish the work of making disciples by teaching obedience to the commandments of Christ. Of course the body of Christ lacks spiritual power because of universal corruption caused by unconfessed subtle and blatant sin permeating the lives of American Christians.

Just as the athlete's physical condition is determined by the quality and disciplines of the intake of physical nourishment, so, too, is the Christian's spiritual condition determined by the quality and disciplines of his or her intake of spiritual nourishment, beginning, of course, with the Word of God. Physical exercise and spiritual obedience are the proper subsequent uses of the physical and spiritual power generated from these nourishment resources. Since only 17 percent of Americans read the Bible regularly, we must conclude that a majority of church-going Christians are in a famished and weakened condition spiritually, and many are biblically illiterate, ignorant of the basic principles of Jesus' commandments and are, therefore, undiscipled, ineffective, and unproductive.

Even among the more active "Bible believing" denominations and churches, a misguided leadership is engaged in a massive waste of Christian resources as they continue to pour time, energy, and financial giving into the goals of obsolete paradigms of "evangelical proclamation." If, for the last thirty years, all of these resources had been invested in Jesus' clear and definitive instructions on how national character is changed—spiritually, effectively, and productively—by teaching obedience to his commandments, our nation today would not be in its present moral dilemma.

Pursuit of "decisions" instead of "making disciples by teaching obedience to everything Jesus has commanded" may be the Christian version of our modern cultural obsession with instant gratification. Claims of quick-decision victories replace Jesus' call for the personal involvement and long-term commitment required to make disciples by teaching obedience. Such surrender by Christians to the superficial tempo of modern culture may explain why we have a national condition where 85 percent of the population are believers with only 17 percent reading the Bible regularly, producing an undiscipled nation in a state of spiritual and moral collapse. In Jesus' Great Commission instructions, the making of a disciple was an inclusive plan.

Being taught obedience included a decision-making process. These were not separate and mutually exclusive considerations, an idea unbiblically promoted and erroneously embraced today. The words *disciple* and *discipling* are very biblical. The word *decisions* is not used in the context of conversion. While proclaiming the "Good News" is solidly biblical, in the historically unique circumstances of the dominant Christian presence in the United States, it must be accomplished within the framework of the discipling process.

Thankfully, not one of these sad conditions is impervious to the remedy prescribed by Jesus in his commandment in John 8:31–32, "If you continue in my word, then you are my disciples indeed and you will know the truth and the truth will set you free." Open-minded, daily, prayerful study of the Word of God will eliminate the immobilizing weaknesses existing in the body of Christ and prepare each individual for the national discipling initiatives required to restore American culture to a state of discipled righteousness. This will result from Christian understanding of and obedience to the biblical goal-achievement system of Vision, Mission, and Strategies.

Among the first paradigm shifts important to productive rapport with the local print media takes place when Christians abandon and replace their unbiblical, negative, and adversarial attitudes with recognition that this is a group of individuals and neighbors doing their job as best they can. God loves each of these souls and Jesus gave his life for every one of them. In truth, they must be seen as potential allies, and Christians should be praying for each of them by name.

From their inception some three years ago, the Church Writing Groups in Lansing have been listing the local staff reporters and editorial writers and praying for them individually. Last fall, the first Church Writing Group conference was held at Michigan State University, sponsored by the Amy Foundation.

Fifty conferees attended from Michigan, Indiana, and Illinois. Several speakers presented seminars on various aspects of discipling through writing in the local secular media. The most popular speaker, eliciting the greatest number of questions, the speaker imparting the most practical, helpful information was Marcia Van Ness, assistant editorial-page editor from the *Lansing State Journal*. Her subject was, "Qualities Producing a Superior Letter to the Editor." For more than an hour she answered the technical, hands-on, working questions that had puzzled conferees. Conversely, she also dealt with those characteristics in writing that turn off the editors. In all the years I've attended Christian Writer conferences, her workshop was one of the most productive I've witnessed. In fact, this was the first open exchange between those committed to discipling through secular-print media and a working newspaper editor I have seen. The exchange was educational, informative, helpful, practical, unbiased, objective, and an extraordinary writer-learning experience.

Pen and Sword, the Church Writing Group newsletter, is being sent to several on the *Lansing State Journal* reporting staff. Recently we received a call from one of the columnists advising us that she had been receiving our newsletter and had seen the promotion of our new video. She told she was going to have some extra space in her column, and she needed additional information so she could tell her readers about the Church Writing Group Movement and inform them of the new video available to help them get started.

Christians! Those of you who love the Lord, who are concerned for the future of our nation, think through very carefully the dynamics and biblical truth at work in the previous paragraphs. God is easily capable of discipling our nation. Jesus commanded us to disciple our nation. He would not command us to do that which is impossible. Pray for a discipled nation. Then pray, "Here am I, Lord, send me."

TALK-RADIO: TODAY'S MISSION FIELD

Radio as a discipling medium has a disadvantage to both newspapers and television. Measured by the volume of advertising revenue attracted, radio comes in a distant third behind the television and newspaper industries. However, results from the last congressional election bear witness that radio is becoming a powerful new influence providing an effective alternative to the TV network news: Talk-radio. A regular listener recently called Rush Limbaugh and thanked him for the marvelous financial return on investments she'd made in companies sponsoring his show. This incident has a symbolic significance far beyond its more obvious meaning. It speaks to growing audiences and increased advertising revenues for talk-radio. A major ideological connection had been made between talk-radio personalities and an expanding audience discovering its political moorings through articulate definition of issues from a conservative viewpoint. Such a media-conservative connection has rarely been accomplished in mass broadcast communication.

While Christians have access to broadcast radio through station ownership, such stations invariably seem to evolve into a "singing to the choir" experience because they are usually listener supported. However, our judgment may be premature and unduly skeptical. Perhaps we should raise our expectations and sense of mission regarding Christian radio-station owners and managers. An exciting prospect is to imagine what the listening audience might hear from such radio stations if owners and managers were committed to doing all in their power to present to our heavenly Father in 2025, the United States, a discipled nation.

How would the character of Christian radio be changed if those responsible for programming direction were imbued with the biblical sense of discipling VISION, MISSION, AND STRATEGY presented in the pages of this book? Nothing is wrong with Christian station managers engaging in consequential thinking that includes an element of spiritually enlightened self-interest. After all, it was Jesus who articulated the spiritual law of reciprocity. "Give, and it will be given to you. A good measure, pressed down, shaken together and running over, will be poured into your lap. For with the measure you use, it will be measured to you" (Luke 6:38). Effective and productive teaching of discipling in three modes (one-on-one, through the church, and through the local print media) would have a singular, predictable result: increased numbers of discipled Americans. Returned to the Christian station, empowered with such biblical vision would be enlarged listening audiences. Listeners imbued with discipling VISION, MISSION, and STRATEGY. Increased gifting revenue. A station staff united in mission to achieve the goal of a discipled United States.

Opportunities for local believer discipling in secular radio do not exist as they do in newspaper journalism, that is, except for the few call-in talk shows at the local level. The question must be raised with Gallup studies showing two powerful undercurrents at work in our society as being "an intensified search for meaning in life and an intensified search for meaningful relationships rising out of loneliness," why is there not more creative imagination at work in Christian circles to address these issues? Why not a format of "talk-radio," centered around a bright, engaging, enjoyable, Christian personality presenting a biblical response to the urgent issues of the day? The talk-show host would possess a strong sense of discipling mission supported by sensitivity to where the caller is spiritually. With an understanding of the need to communicate religious issues in the secular language of contemporary culture, the host totally avoids fluent evangelical and fellowship Christianese.

Christian leadership, denominational and otherwise, must accept a large degree of accountability for the dulled level at which sense of discipling mission exists in the average believer's order of priorities. Where there is little or no sense of discipling mission, there will be little or no spiritually enlightened, creative imagination in development of secular talk-radio from a Christian perspective.

Still, the same laws of business survival motivate local secular radio-station owners and managers as they do all those responsible for producing satisfactory financial results in any business enterprise. *Profit* is an honorable word, not only in a free-enterprise system but also in the Bible. "All hard work brings a profit, but mere talk leads only to poverty" (Proverbs 14:23). The market need exists in the intensified search for meaning in life and the search for meaningful relationships identified by Gallup studies as two powerful undercurrents at work in our society. Christian leadership must increase its effort to understand, define, and effectively provide a discipling response to these deep, universal yearnings in American lives.

CABLE TV: CHANNEL SURF FOR CHRIST

Television is in a class by itself. Surely a grievous disappointment in its failure to live up to the high calling of its educational and culture-shaping potential for improving the lives of the viewing audience, TV's track record is dismaying. Nearly all of the 65,000 readers responding to the write-in survey published by *USA Weekend,* June 1995, said TV is too vulgar, too violent, and too racy. "Sexual content tops the list of 'troublesome programming,' with violence second." Written by Dan Olmsted and Gigi Anders and titled, *Turned OFF,* the article reported:

> "The results were not scientific, but they're overwhelming—and make for a comparison with two years ago. Viewers still find TV violence troubling but seem

increasingly concerned about rawness, especially on the networks' prime-time shows.

"Concern over violence remains high, to be sure: 88% of readers who responded to the write-in are 'very concerned' about it, compared with 95% in 1993.

"'We limit our kids' TV viewing because of the violence, and because too much TV of any kind turns their minds to jelly,' says Sue Sherer, forty, of Rochester, NY, a mother of three (ages eleven, nine, and seven) and PTA president who filled out the survey. 'We rob kids of innocence when we expect them to grow up so fast and mirror kids like those on *Roseanne*. I don't want them to be naive, either, but I'd like them to be children. And TV is a great vandal of that.'

"Responding to the concern over vulgarity, *USA Weekend* monitored five evenings of prime-time network TV (8:00–11:00 p.m. ET). We enlisted journalism students from the American University School of Communication in Washington, D.C., who videotaped each program and noted incidents of crude language or sexual situations.

"The result: 370 incidents over five nights—after giving the tube the benefit of the doubt on close calls. 'I was surprised,' said Alan Tatum, one of the AU students who helped us. 'Even on 'family' shows, it almost seems the producers feel they need to throw in bodily humor every so often.'

"Every 8.9 minutes, on average. And 208 incidents— well over half—occurred in 'the family hour.'"

Cable TV holds not only the promise of local access, but in such outstanding offerings like C-span, it is providing the viewing public with alternative TV news sources, breaking the network national news monopoly and doing it with live broadcasts of such happenings as National Press Club speeches and congressional debates. This is television coming into its own.

In Lansing, cable TV is very accessible. The programming department at Continental Cablevision provides channel 37 as a public access channel. Air time on 37 is available on a first-come, first-served basis to anyone who lives in the Continental Cable (CC) service area. CC provides equipment and training so that individuals can produce their own programs. Air time, equipment, or training is free. With larger churches increasingly producing high-quality dramatizations of biblical stories and productions of the biblical events surrounding major Christian holidays, here is another discipling opportunity. Whenever these can be adapted and taped for local television viewing, we are bridging the gap between the church and the local TV-viewing audience.

Some years ago, the Amy Foundation was approached by a local pastor who, with a keen sense of vision, described a Bible study he would like to present on the local public-access channel. After studying the costs and discussing the idea with the station management, we agreed to underwrite the production costs. Over a period of several months, two complete series were produced and taped. They began running regularly.

One Friday morning he called me and asked if he could come over for a few minutes. We sat in my office and chatted. He suggested we pray. As this precious servant of the King bowed his head, he reminded God that the desire of his heart was that when he stood before him in heaven, he would hear his heavenly Father say, "Well done, good and faithful servant." Next morning he was found in his easy chair, where he had peacefully died the evening before. The Bible study series was titled *The Pastors' Corner*, and it ran at irregular intervals for many years after his death.

Americans have a deep hunger for meaning in their lives. Ken Wales, producer of the superb TV series *Christy*, which premiered on CBS on Easter Sunday, 1994, said Americans want more shows like *Christy*. He cited high ratings—especially in the Midwest—where he said *Christy* achieved "Super Bowl Numbers.

Unfortunately, *Christy* was canceled by CBS because of unfavorably demographics of age and urban audiences.

As reported by Will Swaim in the *Religious News Service Bulletin* of February 15, 1995:

> "So long as such shows earn high ratings, you're likely to see more," says John Sheehan, executive director of The Center for Media and Public Policy in Washington, D.C. "They're not going to put shows on or keep them on if they're not commercially successful," Sheehan says.
>
> The success of religious programming like *Christy* is "a recognition of the values of the American people and the mood of the country," Sheehan says. "We're not ever going back to the days of *Ozzie and Harriet* or *Leave It to Beaver.* But we are going to get a truer picture of the way families deal with their problems."

Christians need to mobilize and use innovative methods to make use of the billions of dollars nationally in communication resources available at very little or no cost in their local community. Print media, radio, and television are potentially discipling giants, waiting for the teaching effectiveness of spiritually enlightened use by the children of the Kingdom.

CHAPTER 10

Discipling Self, Family, Church, and Community

OUR PLANE WAS fifteen minutes from touchdown at Los Angeles and I was about to experience one of the most effective five minutes of business communication I'd ever known. Ten years in the building of Russell Business Forms, Inc., I was now on the executive committee of the National Business Forms Association, en route to lead a seminar on management education. Shortly after take-off from Chicago O'Hare, I discovered I was seated next to a vice president of the R. R. Donnelly Co., perhaps the largest printing company in the world. Three hours with a person I quickly recognized as a management genius proved exhilarating. He was friendly and seemed to enjoy our discussion even though I was obviously probing his mind as if there were no tomorrow. Perhaps he was challenged by my voracious appetite for learning the advanced business insight he possessed and willingly shared. I knew this rare opportunity was about to end.

Finally I turned to him and asked, "Tomorrow I will be speaking to a group of presidents and owners of small businesses. If you had only five minutes with these management people, what is the most important advice you could give them?"

He was silent for only a moment as he reflected on the question. Then he turned to me with deep seriousness and said,

"If I were speaking to your group, there are three important principles I would want them to know. (1) In a small business with limited resources, every decision must be made in the light of how it will effect the survival of the enterprise. (2) Management must have a disciplined strategy for the accumulation of retained earnings so they can adapt to the marketing and technological changes taking place in the industry. (3) Management must have a sound and enlightened program for the training and development of their human resources."

As I finished capturing this entrepreneurial feast on paper, I thought of the thousands of small-business failures that might have been averted if their owners possessed, understood, and applied these foundational truths in their struggling businesses. I expressed my gratitude as we parted, and over the years, the wisdom of this brief interlude has aided many hundreds of small businesses in our national association.

Why does this simple story loom so important to me now as we weave this chapter of effective communication related to discipling our nation? I believe all truth has its origin in the Bible. Sound *business* management principles are in reality sound *biblical* management principles. Biblical management principles can be used as effectively by religious organizations as by business. In discipling, problems develop when Christians begin placing their faith in the principle, process, technique, style, or method rather than in God. The important thing is to work for maximum efficiency in method. Wisdom demands the updating and changing of format and style in response to the changing times and culture, but the new process must never replace our dependence on God to produce the desired outcome. Our faith and trust in him must remain focused and steady.

Your first discipling obligation is to your spouse and family, then church family, followed by community and nation. These efforts should be carried out simultaneously. If each of us is obedient, teaching responsibility to family, church, and community, we will reap the harvest of a discipled nation. We are empowered as effective disciplers when we have a prayerful and biblical relationship with God. It begins with a nurtured conviction that Jesus' final discipling instructions were very important to him and, therefore, must be at the core of our desire to serve him in obedience.

FAMILY DISCIPLING—COMMUNICATION IS THE KEY

In marriage and family life, preservation of the family can be equated with survival of the enterprise. Every decision must be made in the light of how it will affect the survival of the family in harmony with biblical truth. Through habitual, daily, prayerful reading of God's Word, retaining and memorizing those passages important to harmonious family communication, his truth becomes so ingrained in us that it subtly dominates our thoughts, words, actions, and behavior. We will come to recognize even unseemly behavior in family relations such as anger, impatience, or unkindness so that we regret it and soon amend it in confession, repentance, forgiveness, and healing. We must exercise self-control to keep such behaviors to an absolute minimum, or totally avoid them because of the emotional scars they may cause.

Our communication interest is in those forces that shape, support, and lead to effective relations and dialogue rather than those factors concerned with mechanics and style. Phyllis and I were married forty-seven years in August 1995. She is one of the most patient, loving people I have ever known. I am impatient and egotistical. Reading Proverbs recently, I discovered I have been a fool for many years. It isn't easy for a vain man to admit being a fool and the need to confess the presence of such a sinful condition over many years is very humbling. "A fool shows his annoyance at once, but a prudent man overlooks an insult" (Proverbs 12:16). The first half of the proverb hurts. Quick to show annoyance has been a disgraceful trait of mine as long as I can remember. God confronted me with the repugnance of that subtle sin on a morning when I fervently prayed for him to help me *know* and *do* what is right. A prudent man does not show annoyance, but rather, overlooks every offense, real or imagined.

Discipling Your Spouse

When two people have been married for nearly forty-seven years and find their love for one another growing deeper, more satisfying, more enjoyable with each passing year, something must be going right in the relationship. Perhaps the greatest contribution I have made to our communication is a committed willingness to be the first to ask forgiveness. Early in our marriage, I resolved I would *always* be willing to be the first to say, "I'm sorry," and ask for forgiveness. Over the years, I have been faithful to that pledge. On the other hand, Phyllis, because of her loving, patient nature, is beautifully restrained in the tensions that develop from time to time. She honors the scriptural assertion that a soft answer turns away wrath. These biblical attitudes work toward peaceful, harmonious relationships. Biblically obedient attitudes of submission to God's will produce an atmosphere where effective communication thrives. No richer source for communication instruction exists outside of God's Word. Imagine the enhanced quality of life in our family, church, community, and nation if each person had been taught, understood, obeyed, and lived in a manner expressing the fruit of the Spirit. Relationships and dialogue would reflect love, joy, peace, patience, kindness, goodness, faithfulness, gentleness, and self-control. The speech of those who are obedient to the cause of discipling our nation must proceed from an inner dominance of the Holy Spirit and reflect the fruit of the Holy Spirit in their lives.

Discipling Through Prayer

We are blessed with five children: Kathy, Vicki, Lori, Jim, and Amy. As children pass through adolescence and late teens, their world is changing so rapidly they have difficulty keeping pace with their ever-changing role in life. Posing the question to each of our children, "What were the family experiences, examples, counseling, and teaching in your growing-up years that made a memorable contribution to your faith? These would be experiences initiated by their mother and me as parents that they would consider 'discipling' in the sense they taught obedience of Jesus' commands and added to their faith.

They thought that prayer time together was the experience creating the most indelible and lasting faith-building impression. They remembered our prayers before each meal and our prayers together as a family before any trip or major family undertaking.

Lori recalled the times she and I prayed together when she was overwhelmed by a serious teen- or young-adult problem. Vividly, she remembers the faithfulness of God's answers to these prayers. These were major faith-building experiences for her.

Jim felt our prayer time together as family was significant in shaping his spiritual walk with God.

Vicki recalls one night as a child, she woke up about three o'clock and came into our bedroom, terribly frightened. She thought she was dying. She recalls wanting us to take her to the hospital; however, we persuaded her to wait just a short time while the three of us prayed, asking God to give us wisdom in the decision and for him to give her peace and healing while we prayed. By the time we finished our prayers, her anxiety had passed and she was ready to go back to bed. As an adult, Vicki was moved when a close friend, divorced, wistfully said to her, "I remember your father saying, 'families that pray together, stay together.'" A passing verbal expression of God's truth remained in this young lady's heart for years.

Amy's prayers reveal an inner peace in her relationship with God. She describes her response to difficult times at school. Going to her room, she prays through the discomforting situation and tells of the good feeling that comes over her as she prays and as she concludes her time with God.

Discipling Through Example

As Jim grew older, he saw the respect Phyllis and I displayed for one another and the obvious high esteem we held for the value of family life. This became increasingly important to him. Our desire to share God's blessings with others impacted his life also.

With Kathy, parental leadership by example produced learning experiences she continues to value today, especially family attitudes of hospitality toward anyone who came to our door and our openness to friends the children frequently brought home. Hospitality is one of Phyllis' gifts identified by the Houts giftedness inventory. Kathy recalls our provision for an apartment for my mother so she could maintain her passion for independence in her final years.

Discipling Through Communication

Kathy remembers an awareness that despite occasional disagreements and differences, these tensions were never permitted to threaten the security and preservation of the family. Apology, forgiveness, and reconciliation were embraced long before hostile positions hardened into permanent antagonisms.

Anger is the destroyer of communication effectiveness. To the child, anger is an adult out of control. Defenseless and completely vulnerable in the face of adult anger, a child experiences fear, bewilderment, loneliness, and abandonment, leaving him emotionally scarred. Anger is the antithesis of the fruit of the Holy Spirit, love, joy, peace, patience, kindness, goodness, faithfulness, gentleness, and *self-control*. Appearing several times in the concordance of my Bible is the phrase, "slow to anger, abounding in love." Its repeated use speaks to the need for love to dominate and overcome anger. A complete summation is presented in Proverbs, "A fool gives full vent to his anger, but a wise man keeps himself under control" (Proverbs 29:11).

CHURCH DISCIPLING—BECOMING ONE IN CHRIST

As I stated earlier, our small church was recently without a pastor for eighteen months. After seven years, our young pastor accepted a call to a denominational church near Seattle, and we began the search for a replacement. After grieving the loss of this young man of God, the quest began. It was not an easy assignment. Our budget is modest. Michigan winters are severe. The church is located in a nontraffic area. The pastor search committee was faithful in their perseverance through several disappointing invitations. God is faithful and, today, we have his pastor serving the congregation in loving obedience.

A remarkable thing happened during our eighteen months without a pastor. Church attendance and membership grew. Yes, there were some obvious factors. We had superb interim pastors, and our departed young leader left us in a very stable situation, well-positioned for growth. More than any other factor, however, was the prayerful godliness with which the congregation met every disappointment, every trial, every setback, and the underlying sense of oneness in Christ that we shared. During a time normally conducive to Satan's attack, we overcame dissension and factions by kindness, goodness, gentleness, and love. Christ-centered communication prevailed during a time when

God's enemy could have enjoyed a series of victories. Here, disciples were communicating effectively. Discipling was being accomplished. Disciples were being made. The Great Commission was being lived out during difficult circumstances.

COMMUNITY DISCIPLING—A DAUNTING TASK

I do not present our marriage, our family, our church, as models. The discipling lesson is that when God is honored, when Jesus is obeyed, when truth is pursued, good things happen. God's will is done on earth as it is in heaven. The chasm between effective community discipling and teaching obedience in family and church settings is wide. Family members know us. Church friends expect some degree of biblical teaching in a religious environment. In both situations we know what to expect because the situations are familiar to us. The leap from these semi-hospitable, culturally familiar surroundings into the skeptically indifferent realm of the prince of this world is a formidable move for most Christians. Because of biblical illiteracy with little or no discernment for God's truth, few Christians realize the precarious position in which they place themselves by their unwillingness to be engaged in discipling the secular community. Fear of rejection by the world is not an acceptable excuse for being ashamed of Jesus Christ. Jesus said, "If anyone is ashamed of me and my words, the Son of Man will be ashamed of him when he comes in his glory and in the glory of the Father and of the holy angels" (Luke 9:26). Mark quotes Jesus, "If anyone is ashamed of me and my words in this adulterous and sinful generation, the Son of Man will be ashamed of him when he comes in his Father's glory with the holy angels" (Mark 8:38). The cost of being ashamed of Jesus is high.

How do we overcome the timidity, the fear, the sense of inadequacy that leaves us, individually and collectively, in cultural isolation while Satan prowls about like a roaring lion devouring the spiritual infants we have led to Christ and then shamelessly abandoned on the doorstep of his world?

Truth! "What is truth?" (John 18:38). Pilate was face-to-face with truth in all its purity and power when he asked the question. He was haunted by his desire to know. It dominated his being in that moment. He must have sensed its presence. His question went unanswered.

Truth is the mind of God revealed in his holy Word. Truth is the mind of God revealed in the living example of Jesus Christ. Truth is the mind of God revealed to us by the Spirit of truth, the Holy Spirit. Truth is the mind of God being revealed in the life of an obedient Christian. Truth—more than any other power—is feared by Satan and all of those living in obedience to him. Truth uplifted in the person of Jesus Christ by his obedient disciples is the authority empowering the teaching of obedience to a community. It can begin by the simple declaration of a biblical principle applied to a current issue and reinforced with Scripture. This can be done in a hundred different ways by the Christian serving in the mission of discipling this nation.

Christians must recognize new paradigms relating to truth.

Possession of truth means nothing, absolutely nothing, until it is expressed in lovingkindness. Accumulation of truth means nothing. Endless pursuit of additional truth means nothing. Mere possession of truth is equivalent to a dusty Bible, unopened and lifeless, resting on an abandoned shelf. Since the biblical definition of wisdom is *knowing* and *doing* what is right, it becomes obvious that knowing and possessing truth is meaningless without its use in living, loving obedience. Since Jesus is the living Word, the way, the truth, and the life, his passion for obedience to his Father exemplified fulfillment of truth. As the living Word, Jesus possessed all truth. Even so, the purpose of truth was only accomplished by his living obedience to everything he himself commanded. The power of truth is fulfilled in *being an obedient disciple, and making disciples by teaching obedience of everything Jesus had commanded us.*

Christians need to overcome their fear of discipling by getting off the center mark and jumping into it. A prevailing myth handcuffing and immobilizing Christians into dust-covered neutrals is that one must possess near-perfect understanding of truth in order to qualify for the joyful work of making disciples. Nothing could be further from the truth. Speaking recently at a gathering, I was asked the question, "My husband and I are being discipled now. At what point will we have sufficient maturity to being discipling others?" She obviously wanted to be involved in discipling others. With tenderness, I said to her, "I believe that within the hour of a person's becoming a Christian, one is not only qualified to begin discipling but also should be encouraged to do so. As a new Christian, you are now the world's greatest authority, based on your own personal experience. You possess some understanding of the truths leading to your decision, and you will speak with joy, conviction, authority, and persuasive power about your personal experience. To wait until you are qualified or understand more or are better-prepared are all procrastinating excuses used by millions of Christians to continue doing nothing while all around them, the moral collapse of our nation accelerates. You, precious one, are more than ready at this very moment." She smiled softly in agreement as she answered, "I thought you might say that."

Are we advocating not studying the Bible? Of course not. We are to continue in the Word. We are to pursue knowledge and wisdom. However, we are not to use our lack of faith and courage as a procrastinating excuse for the endless pursuit of more understanding. Jesus said, "Therefore go." It is a simple, clear instruction to use what you have today plus what he brings, "all authority in heaven and on earth," and with his everlasting presence you are sufficiently prepared today.

Community discipling can begin one-on-one. We can disciple fellow employees off-hours, not on employer's time. We can implement neighborhood Bible studies. Books and subscriptions to Christian publications can be shared. We can start Church Writing Groups. We can instigate discipling think tanks among Christians to develop discipling uses for public service time on radio and television. God delights in using the most unqualified among us for accomplishing seemingly impossible tasks. He asks three things: faith, obedience, and love. If you claim faith and express it in obedience and action, he will honor such love, beyond imagination.

Effective communication proceeds from understanding of Vision's goal, Mission's work, and Strategy's plan. The substance to be communicated is *truth*, which is the mind of God revealed by the Holy Spirit in his Word, lived out in the obedience of his Son.

Never in world history has a nation been as favorably positioned for discipling as is the United States today. Everything is in place. The spiritual universe awaits the Christian response to this defining moment. A glimpse of God's glory defined in the Scripture, "Your kingdom come, Your will be done on earth as it is in heaven," will be examined in our eleventh and concluding chapter, *Great Commission Obedience and the New Nation*.

CHAPTER 11

Great Commission Obedience and the New Nation

WHERE IS THE first discipled nation? If the Vision of God is defined in the long-term goal of "Your kingdom come, Your will be done on earth as it is in heaven." If Jesus defines the central work of Mission to achieve the goal of Vision, and in his *final* instructions, clearly establishes this work to be "Make disciples of all nations teaching them to obey everything I have commanded you" (Matthew 28:19–20), *where is the first discipled nation?*

Two thousand years have passed since Jesus gave these final instructions. In God's perfect timing, an obedient remnant will come forth, captured by the excitement, the joy, the challenge, the demanding disciplines of obedience to biblical Vision, Mission, and Strategy and will fulfill the commandments required for a discipled nation. To the biblically discerning student of history, obviously the United States is a nation incredibly blessed by God. As a nation founded by his people, we have proven the amazing productive capacity of an economy powered by the free-enterprise system. God has enabled us to demonstrate to the world how, under this system, a nation with less than 5 percent of its population engaged in agriculture, can feed itself, sell food in foreign markets, and give generously from its surpluses. In little more than 200 years, we have emerged as the world's only superpower, that is, a world leader in both economic and military strength. Now we must become the world leader in biblical obedience. We must set the international example of a people who understand truth, which is the mind of God, revealed in his Word, revealed in the *obedient* life of his Son Jesus Christ, and revealed through the Spirit of Truth, which is the Holy Spirit, and finally to be revealed in the obedience of a discipled people. We must not only show the world that we understand truth to be the revealed mind of God, but we are a people whose first love is to live exemplary lives in obedience to the disciplines of biblical truth.

Long before the United States became a nation, the people occupying this land were devoted to their faith in God. Their faith was characterized by their passionate desire to be *obedient* to their heavenly Father. This passion for obedience is the distinguishing difference between their faith and the faith of today's American Christian. God has not given up on our nation. He is presenting American Christians the magnificent opportunity to honor him in obedience to his Son, Jesus Christ, by enlisting in the grandest of all causes, *The United States, a discipled nation in this generation*.

Imagine the entire body of Christ in America suddenly discovering and understanding the profound implications in the magnificent proclamation victory God has given them. Eighty-five percent of all Americans believe in the life, death, resurrection, and spiritual existence of Jesus Christ. Eighty-five percent believe in the divine nature and supernatural qualities of Jesus Christ. The American situation is unique in that no leading nation in world history has gospel proclamation been as effectively achieved as in the United States at the close of the twentieth century. When the jailer asked Paul and Silas the most important question of his life, they responded with the most important answer he would ever hear. "He then brought them out and asked, 'Sirs, what must I do to be saved?' They replied, 'Believe in the Lord Jesus, and you will be saved—you and your household'" (Acts 16:30–31). Eighty-five percent of Americans believe in the Lord Jesus. American Christians are at a defining moment in history. We have arrived at a crossroads. Will we accept by faith what scientific polling data establishes as reality? Will we recognize the validity of the biblical definition for the qualifying belief of these newly recognized brothers and sisters and their place in the family of Jesus Christ? Or will we fall back on the shallowness of our convictions, the vanity of our exclusiveness, and the ignorance of our biblical illiteracy and, in human judgment, cynically reject the qualifying belief of these brothers and sisters in Jesus Christ? If the Christian choice is continuation of the abandonment of these spiritual infants to the merciless material and carnal assault of the Enemy, we will answer for our shameful decision on a day of divine judgment when God's perfect and holy justice will be administered!

Instead of turning our backs on these lambs of God, let faith prevail across the land! Travel with me through an imaginary scenario where American believers suddenly recognize and claim with astonishment and joy this glorious proclamation victory and launch a thirty-day celebration of praise and thanksgiving. Nourished by the Holy Spirit, the total joy of celebration generates a spontaneity of unity within churches, between denominations, between races and ethnic groups, and across the entire body of Christ in America. In the joy of Christ-centered victory, broken families are restored, wounds are healed, differences resolved, and ancient animosities forgiven. American heroes of the faith are admired and extolled. Their biblical qualities serve as a revealing mirror and, toward the end of the month, exhilaration turns to sobering questions regarding our nation's declining moral character. "With all this widespread belief in Jesus, how can we as a nation be in the advanced stages of moral decline?" This is the most persistent, perplexing, demanding, question of all. Its paradox dominates conversations. This national contradiction becomes the central issue of Bible studies and prayer gatherings. God is not indifferent. He hears the agony of their perplexity. He feels their compassion. He sees their tears.

Our heavenly Father is a prayer-answering God. Spiritually imparting truth, the Holy Spirit discloses the answer simultaneously to many. Our heavenly Father has given us a magnificent proclamation victory. We have responded with a monumental *discipling* failure! We have all this belief, this acceptance of truth, but it is not discipled, *obedient* belief. After thirty days, the celebration turns to mourning. Grieving over the plight of millions of believers, abandoned as spiritual infants, the body of Christ in America enters a thirty-day period of mourning, fasting, confession, and repentance.

The spirit of God presents two major panoramas of sin and wickedness to the believers. First is the wickedness of the world. Unfaithfulness and the tragedy of adultery. Broken homes and wounded children. More than half the children of America living out the greatest fear of their lives: losing one or both of their parents before they are eighteen. Scarred forever, fearful of rejection from commitment, they live out lonely lives, rarely if ever experiencing the peace of a faithful marriage and the fulfillment of a loving family. Children having children. Teen pregnancies become rampant as government imposes sex education at younger and younger ages, a teaching process devoid of values. The American male is spiritually wimpy. Vicariously achieving a macho self-image through the TV heroics of his favorite football team, he relieves the suppressed guilt of his spiritual cowardice and separation from God by abusing his wife and children emotionally or physically or both. Strident feminism is rampant. Women are abandoning their natural role of homemaker, caretaker, and developer of the spiritual character of the next generation. They are submitting themselves to the vanity of personal ambition and forfeiting the joy of later years surrounded by the love of expanding family expressed in the lives of children and grandchildren. Addiction to drugs, alcohol, pornography, and the resulting evil of uncivilized behavior is presented to Christians of this generation.

As the tragedy of increasing American decadence is held up for all believers to see, the Holy Spirit presents a fearful revelation to the children of God. "This is your doing. You are responsible for this debacle of national wickedness. This is not a condition caused by the media or the movies. It is not a failure of the arts and entertainment; it does not come forth from either Democrats or Republicans, liberals or conservatives. *This national shame is a direct result of your failure, my children, to be obedient disciples and to make disciples by teaching obedience to everything Jesus has commanded you!* The disgraceful moral condition of our nation is the direct result of the spiritual bankruptcy of the Christian community in the United States!

Then the Spirit of Truth reveals the second panorama of sin, the wickedness and hypocrisy of the children of the Kingdom. Here the panorama changes from the blatant sins of the world to the subtle sins of the Christian community. The scenario becomes noticeably darker. Subtle sins are the favored strategic playground of the master planner of the forces of evil. The devious nature of subtle sins renders them nearly impervious to detection, discovery, and elimination by those deceived by the vanity of their personal self-righteousness. Satan glories in the unrepented subtle sins of the influential who dominate the churches and denominations of the Christian community. The strategic value and evil nature of these subtle sins exists in their ability to divert and waste critical discipling resources, misdirected energy, time, and goodwill. They work at the seat of power in the vain personal ambition of those in the church. They feed the denominational vanities and provincialism of denominational leadership. Always, always, and always, the strategy of the master planner of the evil kingdom is to divert, distract, and redirect resources and attention from the central work of the children of the Kingdom, *which is to make disciples by teaching obedience of everything Jesus has commanded us.*

Because of their insidious nature, they go unconfessed and unrepented, leaving the body of Christ in America under the domination of the universal unconfessed subtle sin, *the vanity of self-righteousness.* This sweeping unconfessed sin is draining spiritual power, effectiveness, and productivity from American believers. As the scales fall away from believers' eyes, they humble themselves and pray; they seek his face, and they turn from their wicked ways. God hears from heaven, He forgives their sin and begins healing their land.

Among the greatest blessings and strengths of the church at the close of the twentieth century is the scriptural knowledge and teaching giftedness of Christian pastors. In a study conducted by Barna Research Group, Ltd., and presented in the book *Today's Pastors* by George Barna, 85 percent of pastors rate themselves good or excellent in scriptural knowledge. Eighty-three percent rate themselves as good or excellent in the ministry of teaching. These two categories were given the highest scores in the eleven areas of ministry effort covered in the pastor self-evaluation. Supporting these Great Commission strengths was another study, The Primary Joys of Pastoring. Here pastors reported their greatest ministry joy is in preaching-teaching, discipling people, and evangelism. These studies tend to support our conclusion that Christian clergy are well-positioned for their critical role in a new twenty-first century era of discipling our nation in this generation. What pastors see as their greatest strengths, the activities from which they derive their keenest joy, are precisely those gifts of highest priority called for in the grand mission of Jesus, discipling our nation in this generation.

Since Jesus defined what God has clearly established as his vision for the entire church, "Your kingdom come, Your will be done on earth as it is in heaven," and Jesus has clearly established his mission for the entire church, "Make disciples by teaching obedience of everything I have commanded you," the pastor's central role is not visionary leadership (positions already occupied by the Creator and his Son), but rather discipler, teacher, and manager. Together with enlightened lay leaders, local strategy, i.e., organized, practical plans for discipling (teaching obedience) of individuals, families, church members, attendees, and community, are developed around the giftedness of the congregation under prayerful solicitation of and leading by the Holy Spirit.

Because of the tremendous productive leverage in discipling reachout, every one of the 350,000 Christian churches in the United States should include a Church Writing Group in its package of discipling strategies. Last week, Tuesday, August 1, 1995, the local newspaper with a daily circulation of approximately 72,000, published a letter to the editor from me. They titled it, *Appreciate Headlines*. It read, "Integrity of the headlines on the editorial pages is one of the many qualities of the *Lansing State Journal* I appreciate. Never misleading, without bias or prejudice, it gets right to the heart of the issue being presented.

"Such objectivity is reassuring and always speaks to character of purpose. The consistency with which this is accomplished is especially pleasing when you consider the diversity of views expressed in letters to the editor and Point of View columns.

"With great wisdom, the apostle Paul applauds this quality in these words:

' . . . a workman who does not need to be ashamed and who correctly handles the word of truth.'

"I appreciate the confidence with which I can pursue the headlines of my interest on the editorial pages of the *Lansing State Journal*."

It was signed, James Russell, President, The Amy Foundation.

Two days later in the Point of View column, Terry Hart, a leader of one of the local CWG's had a 600-word piece published. Rarely in secular publishing do you see the boldness of the large headline proclaiming, "Christian Convert Shares Experience," and beneath in smaller type the subtitle read, "After many years of ridiculing believers, he surrenders to Jesus." Following came a powerful, poignant, and persuasive discipling testimony. Surely, the timing of the publication of these two pieces was orchestrated by the Holy Spirit. " . . . if you have faith as small as a mustard seed, you can say to this mountain . . ." (Matthew 17 :20).

The year has become 2025. Since 1996, Jesus has gradually released, through an increasingly obedient American church, the awesome power contained in his possession of "all authority in heaven and on earth." The vital institutions of the nation are transformed. Not a single aspect of American life remains untouched. Not one principle of the Constitution in harmony with the intent of the signers has been violated. With the remarkable achievement of 85 percent of the American people becoming discipled, obedient Christians, the following United States' institutions have become known by these predominant characteristics.

THE CHRISTIAN CHURCH

Across the nation, in more than 90 percent of the churches, the major activity is discipling, teaching obedience of everything Jesus has commanded us. The mission statement is the one Jesus defined for every church. It needs no human improvement. It reads like this: "All authority in heaven and on earth has been given to me. Therefore go and make disciples of all nations, baptizing them in the name of the Father and of the Son and of the Holy Spirit, and teaching them to obey everything I have commanded you. And surely I am with you always, to the very end of the age" (Matthew 28:18–20). All of church life is directed toward understanding of and obedience to Jesus' commandments. In harmony with the joy of pastor giftedness, new dimensions of teaching, discipling, and making disciples are discovered and implemented. Prayer life of the church focuses on the discipling needs of individuals, families, church members, attendees, and the community.

The church becomes spiritually and financially prosperous beyond belief. As obedience to biblical truth becomes the norm, tithing also becomes the norm. In obedience to Jesus' commands, tithing is recognized as the minimum giving. Jesus taught the spiritual law of reciprocity. "Give, and it will be given to you. A good measure, pressed down, shaken together and running over, will be poured into your lap. For with the measure you use, it will be measured to you." (Luke 6:38). Soon it is recognized you cannot outgive God. With obedience and righteousness comes discernment and justice. Deepening remorse for the financial plight of pastors and their families leads to congregational generosity long overdue.

As love and compassion replace self-interest, the church once again assumes its biblical responsibility in providing more *truly required* social services than are being currently provided by the government. It does so at a fraction of the former cost. Discipling and caring for the needy go hand in hand. Needs of character and soul are met while administering to the physical needs of the body. Character transformation yields a diminishing national problem of the socially dysfunctional. Each church, in some measure, is actively engaged in carrying out its community discipling mission through local print media, radio, TV, and electronic networking.

THE UNITED STATES CONGRESS

In all of the United States' vital institutions, none seems to have experienced greater change than that which has transformed the congress of the United States. As the attitude of Christians toward the subtle sin in their lives became one of shame, humiliation, confession, and repentance, God blessed their nation with a discernment of righteousness never seen in modern times. With daily study of the mind of God through his Word comes a discernment of truth enabling the electorate to recognize biblical righteousness in the lives and words of others. Political candidates find themselves held up to and compared with God's biblical standard of righteousness.

Gradually the United States Congress became internationally renowned for its wisdom and integrity as it transferred responsibility for social services to the private sector. With increasing sensitivity to their biblical responsibility, 350,000 Christian churches replaced the bureaucratic layered, federal welfare system with a private service system highlighted by a loving compassion for the real needs of the individual. Working relationships between the congress and the executive branch and between congress and the judicial branch were marked more by harmonious productivity than stalemated bickering. To the joy of its national constituency, the finest ongoing result from congress was creation, development, and passage of legislation honoring biblical principles.

THE JUDICIARY

Growing spiritual character of the American people empowered them to elect presidents of superior judgment.

When added to the approval power of the United States' Congress over appointments to the Supreme Court, a judicial system finally resulted that was highly sensitive to biblical truth. First evidence came when Supreme Court decisions reflected interpretation of legislation in harmony with the spirit of the intent of the framers of the Constitution. Preservation of the sanctity of family life became an obvious goal in the direction of the decision-making process. Even though violence and crime were diminishing rapidly, judicial rulings were aimed at protecting society from the remaining predators and lawless in our culture. Victims of crime were recognized as the injured party, never the criminal. This was accomplished without infringing on the right of the accused for a fair and speedy trial.

PUBLIC EDUCATION

Since nothing in the Constitution prohibits it, and the vast majority of the American people support its implementation, early in the twenty-first century, prayer was returned to the classrooms of the public school system. Because 94 percent of Americans believe in God, vocal opposition was short-lived and the comforting presence of his divine being was soon evident in the behavioral changes of the students.

Major curriculum changes took place as biblical values were emphasized and taught. Bureaucratic layers of administration were eliminated. Curriculum was revamped to prepare students scholastically to function successfully in the real world. Parents from all backgrounds became actively involved, providing biblical, real-world oversight to the entire educational process. Teachers were held strictly accountable and were evaluated by test scores designed to show the learning progress of their students. The tenure system protecting and shielding mediocrity was abolished.

NEWS MEDIA

Ideological balance and absence of personal bias are major changes observed between the improvements of news presentation in the 2020s and coverage provided in the 1990s. Sense of fairness has become one of the prevailing characteristics of godliness emerging in the United States as a discipled nation. Equally gratifying, as quality of life improved for everyone, a dramatic change in the nature of the news unfolded. Events of worthy example of inspirational value, of discipling character, begin to overshadow the opposite. This resulted not only from a choice of what truly constitutes news but also from a changing frequency of occurrence.

Kingdom advancement becomes news! In a discipled nation, gains in the priorities of God are newsworthy, and news volume of Kingdom advancement exceed victories of evil.

ENTERTAINMENT AND THE ARTS

As obedience and righteousness exalts our nation, the fields of entertainment and the arts emphasize that which is true, noble, right, pure, lovely, admirable, excellent, and praiseworthy. It is difficult to imagine a field where greater transformation takes place than in the hearts, minds, and souls of the writers creating the material intended to inspire, entertain, captivate, and uplift their audiences. Increasingly their work carries a message of the victory, joy, meaning, and honor in lives where virtue and morality are modeled and uplifted. The creative effort of writers living in obedience always leaves the patron uplifted, inspired, and motivated in harmony with biblical truth.

FAMILY

A nation will not become discipled unless the family has been taught obedience first. May God forever bless the American woman for her courageous, faithful willingness to stand in the gap, holding her family together as best she can while the men of this nation pursued the vanities of their spiritual ignorance in the last half of the twentieth century, and finally as it drew to a close, they came to their senses. Can anyone doubt the silent, grateful, prayers of thanksgiving in the hearts of hundreds of thousands of women across our nation as their husbands, many reluctantly, but Spirit-led, went to their first Promise Keepers' meeting?

Again the year is 2025. A spirit of love, harmony, and purpose has descended upon the family as fathers once again accepted their scriptural responsibility in providing biblical and spiritual leadership. A hunger and thirst to know the mind of God and to pursue its revelation in his Word has become a central motivation. Outward joy and inward peace as spiritual leader of a loving family brings the American male a dimension of servant leadership and quality of life he never dreamed existed. To display these biblical attributes in the public eye with serenity and courage without vanity or shame, he knows, is to serve God with love and humility. He is finally at peace with himself, his family, and with his heavenly Father.

Wives and mothers are revered and honored as they work to shape the spiritual character of the next generation in their critical role as maker of the home. Spiritual righteousness of children is nurtured as they are biblically trained in the way they should go. Fathers and mothers are honored by their children as the mind of God is applied in their lives through the wisdom of their parents.

There is rejoicing in heaven as the United States of America becomes the first discipled nation!

PERSONAL OBEDIENCE IS REQUIRED TO MAKE IT HAPPEN!

The United States, a discipled nation, is in perfect harmony with the vision of God, the mission of Jesus Christ, and strategies of discipling truth revealed by the Holy Spirit. Following are disciplines of biblical obedience to which American Christians must submit themselves to make it happen.

1. Pray every day for the United States, a discipled nation in this generation.

2. Praise God every day for the magnificent proclamation victory he has given us. Eighty-five percent of Americans believe in the life, death, resurrection, and spiritual presence of Jesus Christ.

3. Seek to know the mind of God every day by prayerfully reading at least one chapter of his Word. Do this in total surrender to the Spirit of truth's revelation to you. Do not defend vain positions as God speaks directly to you.

4. Pray for the millions and millions of Americans who are spiritual infants, undiscipled lambs, waiting for you to feed them with the nourishment of truth—truth calling for obedience to everything Jesus has commanded us. Pray for those in your family, your church, and your community.

5. Begin a subtle sin inventory of your life today. A discipled nation originates in a righteous remnant. Begin with the sin of the vanity of self-righteousness. Confess in repentance and sorrow the subtle and blatant sins in your life. Do this, hour by hour during the day. Rejoice in the forgiveness and cleansing that leads you into righteousness.

6. Discard the obsolete, ineffective, and unproductive paradigms no longer contributing to the task of discipling our nation as Jesus has commanded. Create new paradigms supporting biblical vision, mission, and strategy for teaching obedience in your family, your church, your community, and nation.

7. Start a Church Writing Group in your church. Subscribe to the CWG newsletter. Employ the strategic leverage of teaching obedience to thousands of Jesus' lambs at one time. Disciple one-on-one as well.

8. Have faith as a grain of mustard seed. You do not need one iota more of knowledge than you possess today to be engaged in discipling today. Your faith supported by your obedient, loving action today will be used by God to disciple our nation. Do not use the procrastinating excuse of the need for more knowledge before you begin. This is Satan's deception to keep you in isolation, doing nothing. Pursue knowledge, but be obediently engaged in teaching obedience as you do it.

9. Support your pastor in his teaching giftedness. Help him embrace and teach the biblical vision, mission, and strategies leading to a discipled nation. *Loan him your copy of this book.*

10. Let all that you do be done in love. The discipling of a great nation begins in the character of love defined in the Great Commandment and is fulfilled in the obedient love described in the Great Commission.

For the American Christian, this must become the grandest of all causes: The United States, a discipled nation in this generation!